A-Z BRIGHTON

CONTENTS

REFERENCE

A Road	**A27**	Cycleway		⚲ ··········
B Road	**B2123**	Fire Station		■
Dual Carriageway		Hospital		Ⓗ
One-way Street		House Numbers (A & B Roads only)		10 / 124
Traffic flow on A roads is also indicated by a heavy line on the driver's left.		Information Centre		𝐢
Restricted Access		National Grid Reference		530
Pedestrianized Road		Park & Ride		Withdean P+↻
Track & Footpath		Police Station		▲
Residential Walkway		Post Office		★
Railway	Level Crossing	...d Limit ...cameras.		30
Built-up Area			...abled	▽
			...Disabled	▽
			...only	▽
Local Authority Boundary		...onal Establishment		▨
Posttown Boundary		Hospital or Healthcare Building		▨
Postcode Boundary	within Posttown	Industrial Building		▨
Map Continuation	12 / Large Scale City Centre 44	Leisure or Recreational Facility		▨
		Place of Interest		▨
Airport	✈	Public Building		▨
Car Park (Selected)	ℙ	Shopping Centre & Market		▨
Church or Chapel	✝	Other Selected Buildings		▢

SCALE

Map Pages 4-43	Map Page 44
1:15,840 4 inches (10.16cm) to 1 mile 6.31cm to 1km	1:7,920 8 inches (20.32cm) to 1 mile 12.63cm to 1km
0 ¼ ½ Mile	0 ⅛ ¼ Mile
0 250 500 750 Metres	0 100 200 300 Metres

Copyright of Geographers' A-Z Map Company Limited

Fairfield Road, Borough Green, Sevenoaks, Kent TN15 8PP
Telephone: 01732 781000 (Enquiries & Trade Sales)
01732 783422 (Retail Sales)
www.a-zmaps.co.uk
Copyright © Geographers' A-Z Map Co. Ltd.
Edition 4 2010

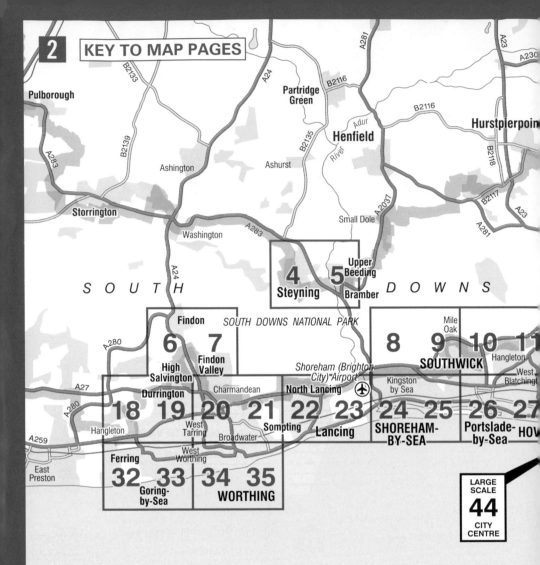

Pulborough

Partridge Green

B2116

Henfield

Hurstpierpoin

Ashington

Ashurst

Adur

River

Storrington

Small Dole

Washington

S O U T H

Upper Beeding

4
Steyning

5
Bramber

D O W N S

Findon

SOUTH DOWNS NATIONAL PARK

Mile Oak

8

9
SOUTHWICK

10

11

Hangleton

6
High Salvington

7
Findon Valley

Shoreham (Brighton City) Airport

West Blatchingt

A27

Durrington

Charmandean

North Lancing

Kingston by Sea

A280

18

19

20

21

22

23

24

25

26

27

Hangleton

West Tarring

Sompting

Lancing

SHOREHAM-
BY-SEA

Portslade-
by-Sea

HOV

A259

Broadwater

West Worthing

East Preston

Ferring

32

33

34

35

Goring-
by-Sea

WORTHING

LARGE
SCALE

44

CITY
CENTRE

ENGLISH

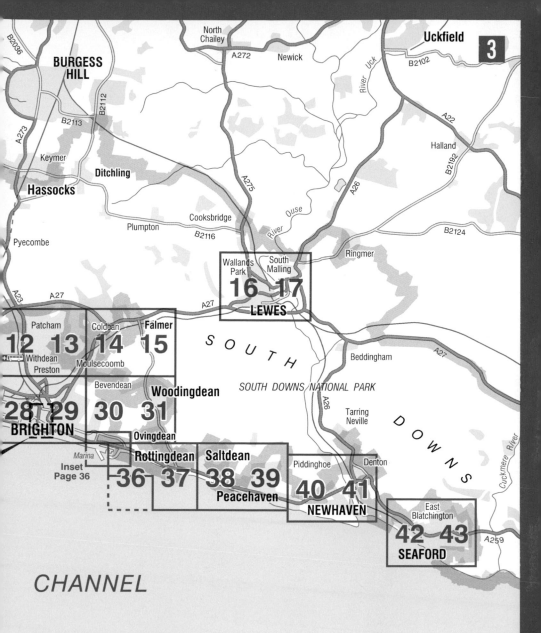

3

UCKFIELD

BURGESS HILL

North Chailey

Newick

River Uck

B2102

A272

A22

Halland

B2112

B2113

A273

Keymer

B2192

Ditchling

A275

Hassocks

Ouse

B2124

Pyecombe

Cooksbridge

River

Ringmer

Plumpton

B2116

A27

Wallands Park

South Malling

A27

16 17

LEWES

Beddingham

A27

Patcham

Coldean

Falmer

S O U T H

A23

A27

12 13 14 15

Withdean

Preston

Moulsecoomb

SOUTH DOWNS NATIONAL PARK

A26

D O W N S

Bevendean

Tarring Neville

Cuckmere River

28 29 30 31

Woodingdean

BRIGHTON

Ovingdean

Marina

Rottingdean

Saltdean

Piddinghoe

Denton

Inset Page 36

36 37 38 39

40 41

East Blatchington

Peacehaven

NEWHAVEN

42 43

SEAFORD

A259

CHANNEL

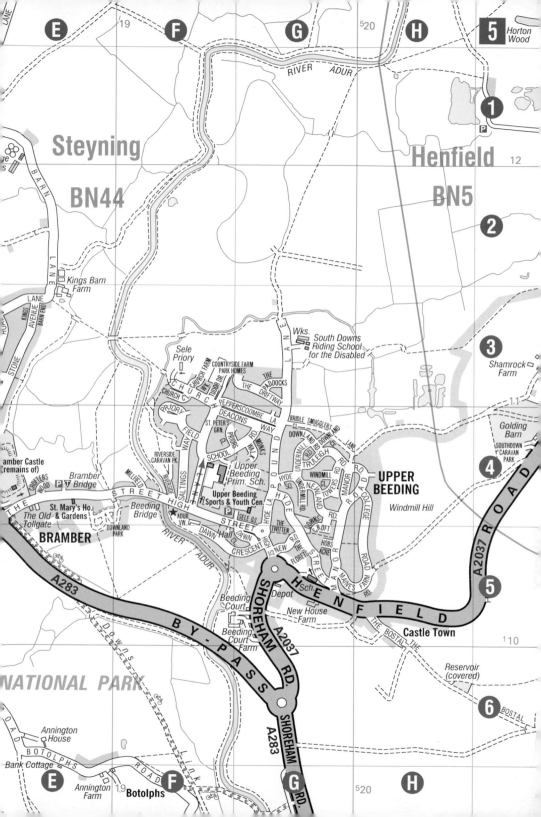

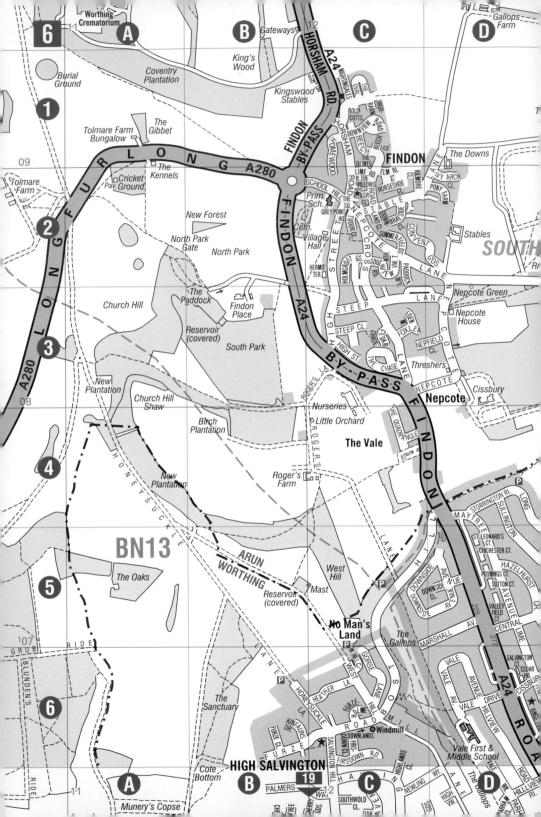

6 A B C D

1

Worthing Crematorium
Burial Ground
Coventry Plantation
King's Wood
Gateways
Kingswood Stables

2

Tolmare Farm Bungalow
The Gibbet
Tolmare Farm
The Kennels
Cricket Pav. Ground
New Forest
North Park Gate
North Park
FINDON
The Downs
SOUTH

3

Church Hill
The Paddock
Findon Place
Reservoir (covered)
South Park
Nepcote Green
Nepcote House
Nepfield CL.
Threshers
Cissbury
Nepcote

4

New Plantation
Church Hill Shaw
Birch Plantation
New Plantation
Nurseries
Little Orchard
The Vale
Roger's Farm

5

BN13
The Oaks
ARUN
WORTHING
West Hill
Reservoir (covered)
Mast
No Man's Land
The Gallops

6

The Sanctuary
Windmill
HIGH SALVINGTON
Cote Bottom
PALMERS **19**
Vale First & Middle School

A B **19** C D

Munery's Copse

E   F   14   G   H   515   **7**

1

Park Brow

Gallops

Stump
Bottom

09

Worthing

DOWNS NATIONAL PARK

ADUR
ARUN

Mill
House

House

Canada Bottom

2

P

3

CISSBURY RING

08

Cissbury
Farm

Hill Barn
Covert

4

Cissbury
Plantation

Shipdens
Holt

Vineyard
Hill

Deep
Bottom

Lychpole
Hill

BN14

Tenants
Hill

5

Sheepcombe
Hanger

Mount Carvey

ADUR
WORTHING

107

MEADOW

AVENUE

HOLLINGBURY

SHEPHERD'S

GARDENS

CISSBURY

6

AV

NDON VALLEY

GARDENS

GARDENS

MEAD

RISE

COOMBE

P

Lib.

WICK

CRES.

THE HEIGHTS

ASHFOLD

E   **WORTHING**   F   **20** 14   G   H

WORTHING GOLF COURSE

(LOWER)

GOLF COURSE

(UPPER)

Reservoir
(covered)

515

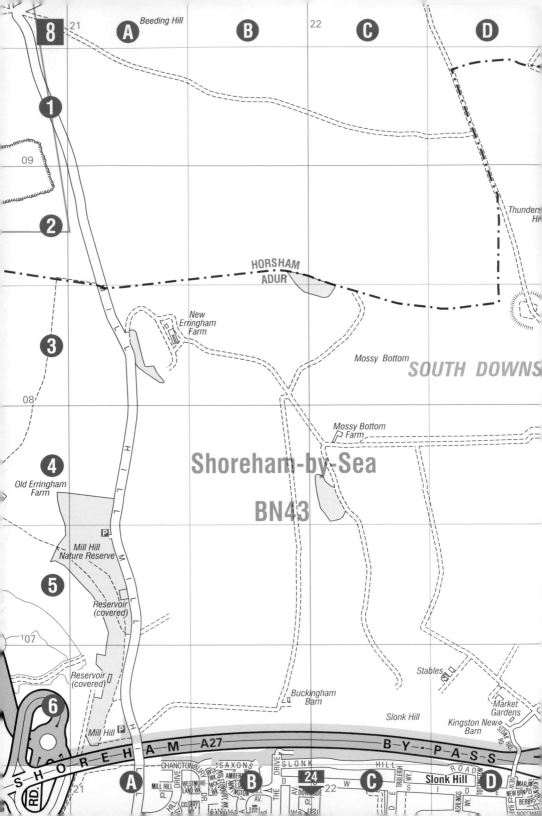

8

21

A Beeding Hill   **B**   22   **C**   **D**

1

09

2

HORSHAM
ADUR

Thunders
Hi

New
Erringham
Farm

3

Mossy Bottom

SOUTH DOWNS

08

Mossy Bottom
Farm

4

Shoreham-by-Sea

Old Erringham
Farm

BN43

P

Mill Hill
Nature Reserve

5

Reservoir
(covered)

107

Stables

Reservoir
(covered)

Buckingham
Barn

Market
Gardens

6

Slonk Hill

Kingston New
Barn

Mill Hill   P

SHOREHAM — A27   BY - PASS

RD.   21

CHANCTONBURY   SAXONS   SLONK
MILL HILL   DRIVE   AMBER   THE DRIVE
CL.   WESTMORE   NGTON   AV.   DOWNSIDE
LAND WK.   AV.   CL.
CISSBRY   WK.   HILL   CL.

A   **B**   **24**   **C** TRULEIGH WY. **Slonk Hill**   **D**

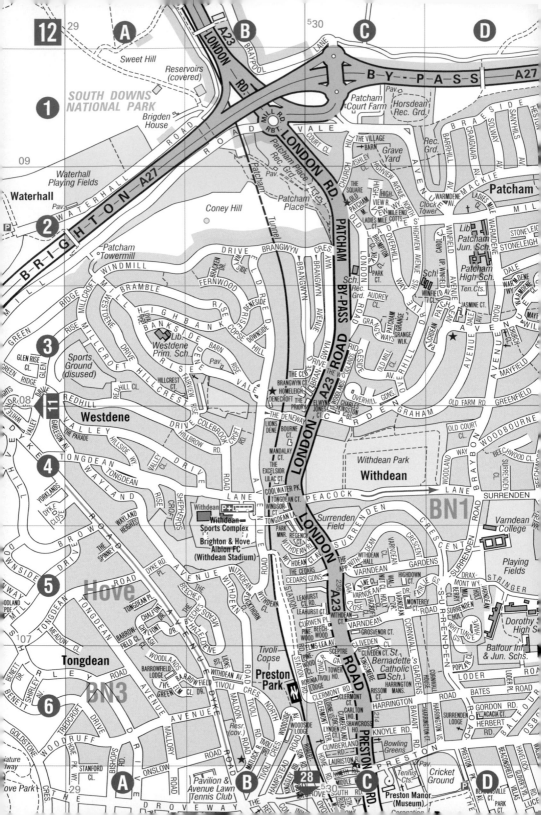

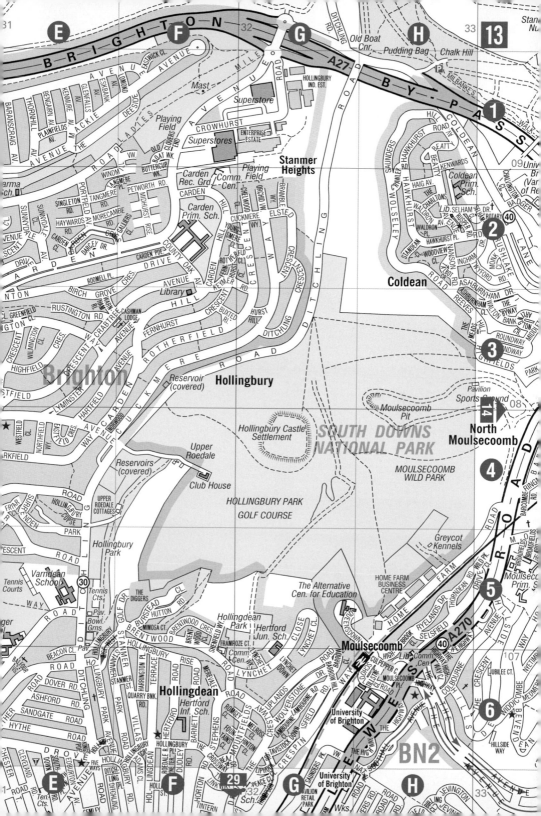

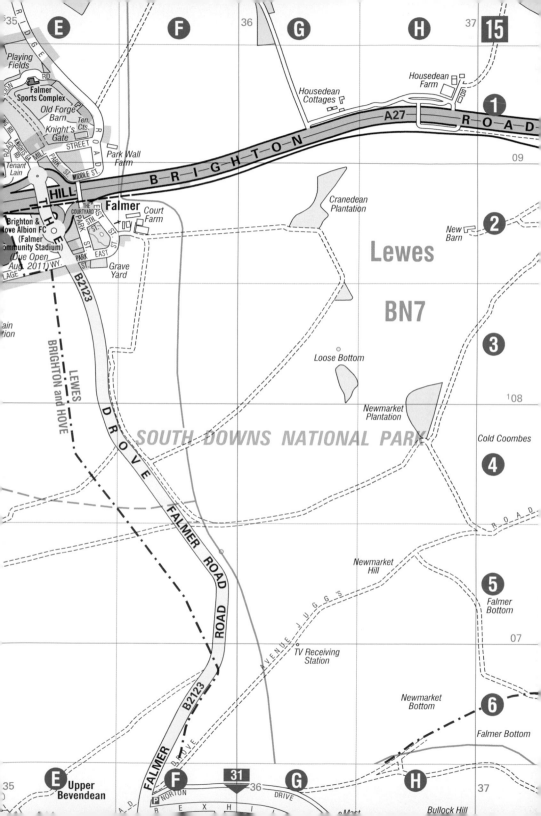

16 39

A   **B**   Offham   540   **C**   The Pells   Cut   **D**

1

OFFHAM A275 ROAD

Offham Hill

Reservoir (covered)

Offham Pits (disused)

Ousedale House

Pellbrook

Chalkpit Cut

Papermill LANDPORT

SOUTH DOWNS NATIONAL PARK

2

THE OLD RACECOURSE

Old Lewes Racecourse

Landport Fork

Landport Bottom

Cuckoo Bottom

11

Landport

OFFHAM ROAD A2029

HIGHDOWN CRES.

HAMSEY CR.

CABURN CR.

SHEEP FAIR

MOUNT

HARRY WINDOVER CRES.

Wallands Prim. Sch.

Wallands Park

BN7

3

FIRLE

EAST DOWNS CL.

NEVILL RD

HILL ROAD

Victoria HOSP.

4

Houndean Bottom

NORTH

MIDDLE WAY

CROSS WY.

SOUTH WAY

SOUTH HWY.

NEWBURY

MILAN GRO.

THE GALLOPS

SPITAL RD.

Reservoir (covered)

Stables

VALENCE

DE MONTFORT Sch.

PRINCE EDWARD'S

WALLANDS PK.

Ousedale CL.

H

A275 ROAD

110

5

HMP LEWES

WESTERN RD.

Houndean Cottages

Houndean Barn

HOUNDEAN RISE

SOUTHDOWN AV.

ROAD

BISHOPS DR.

BARONS DOWN WK.

County Hall

Coun. Offs.

St ANNE'S CRES.

WINTERBOURNE

Cemetery

Rec. Grd.

ROTTEN ROW

St. PANCRAS GDS.

Ashcombe House

BRIGHTON A277 **ROAD**

MONTACUTE

LEWES

WINTERBOURNE LANE

The Folly

JUGG'S ROAD

A27

Southove

SOU

Works

6

BRIGHTON ROAD

ASHCOMBE HOLLOW

Kingston RBT.

A27

CRANEDOWN

Pav.

Stanley Turner Sports Ground

The Cockshut

ASHCOMBE HOLLOW

09

Nan Kemp's Grave

39

A   JUGG'S   **B**   540   **C**   **D**

KINGSTON ROAD

Reservoir

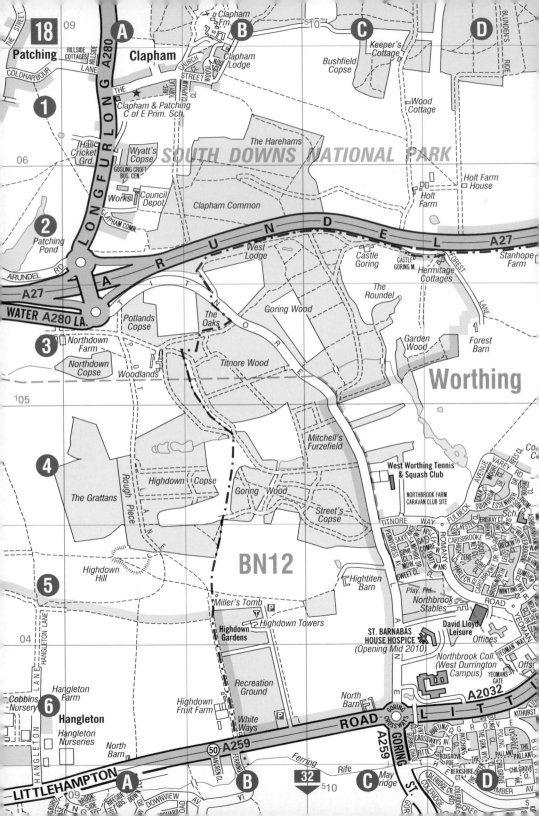

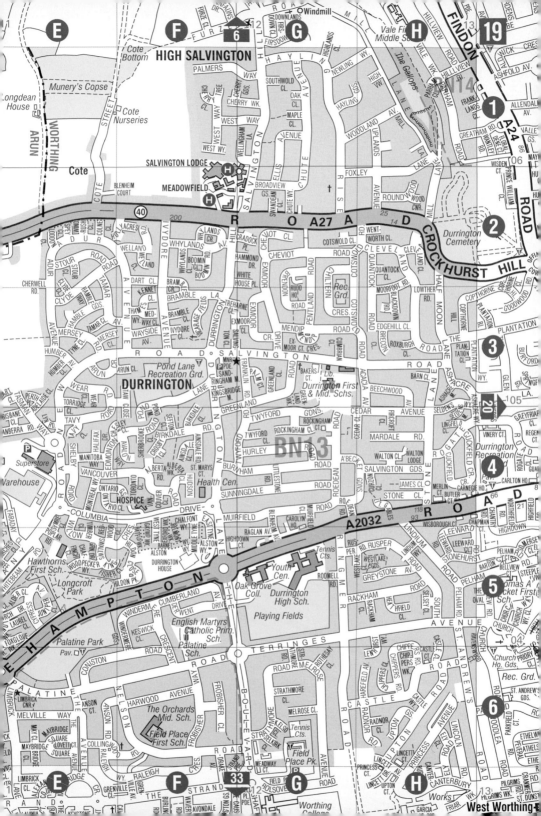

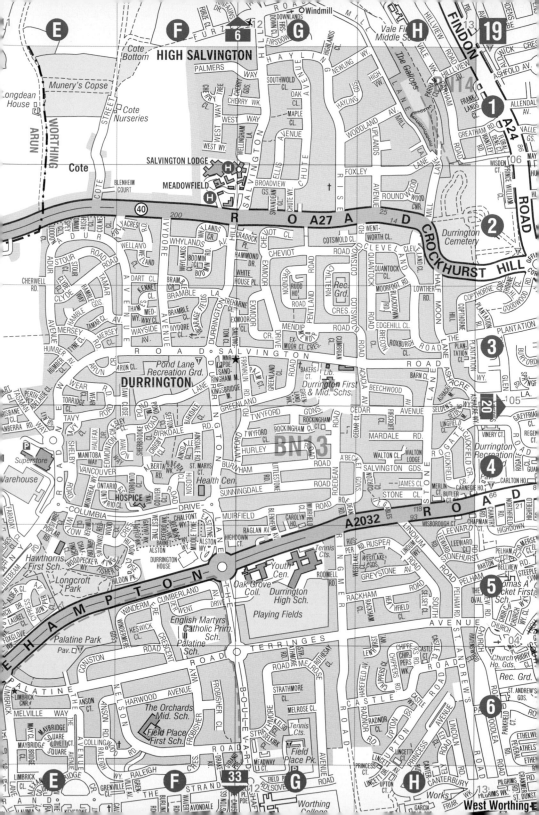

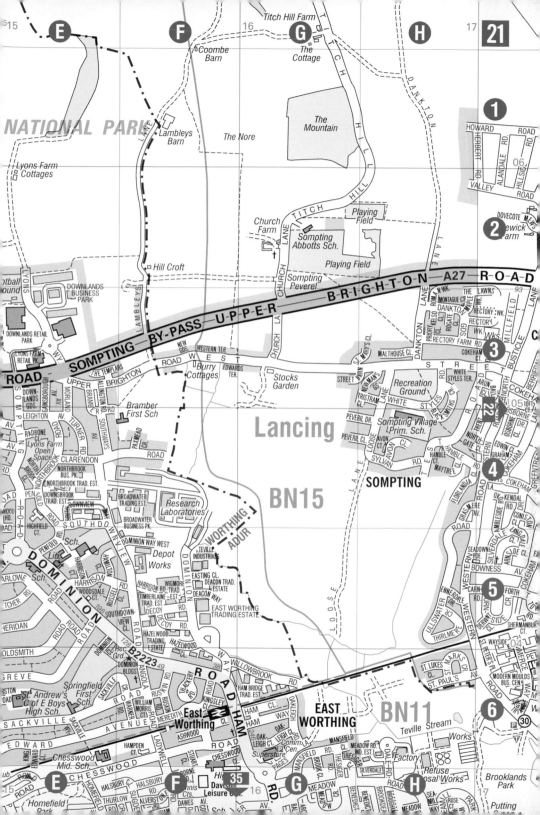

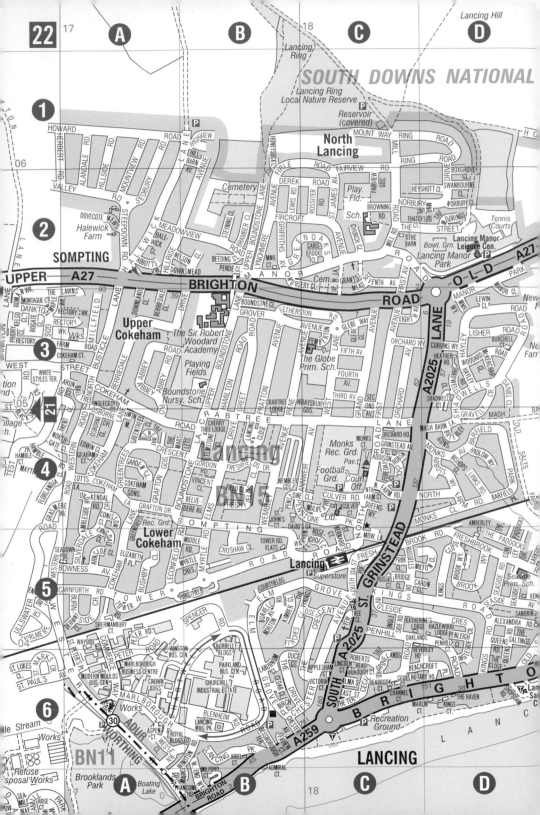

SHOREHAM-BY-SEA

ENGLISH

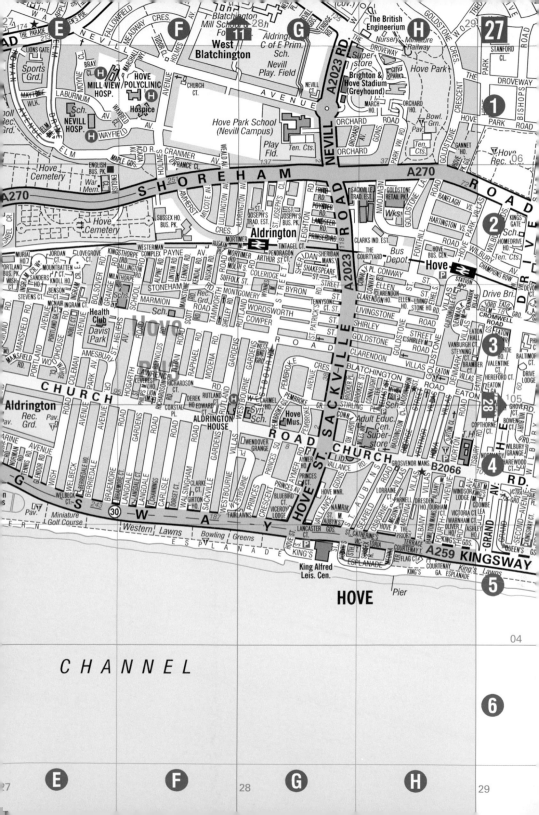

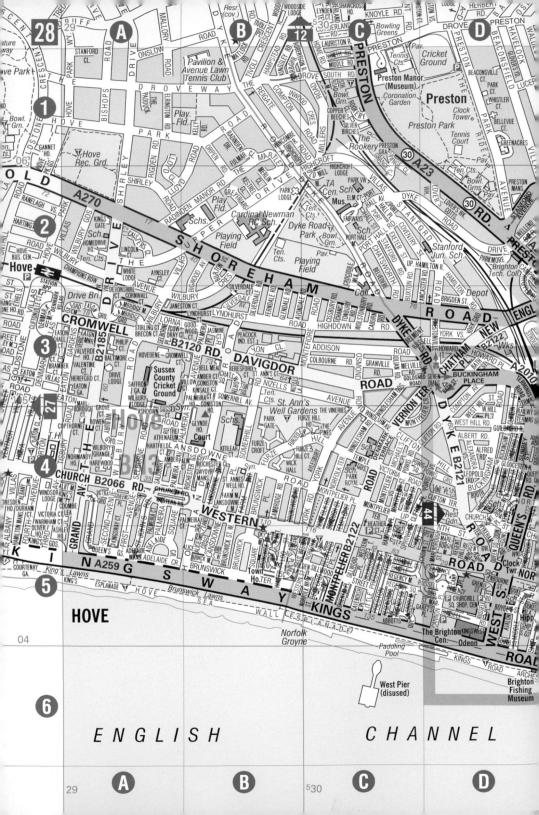

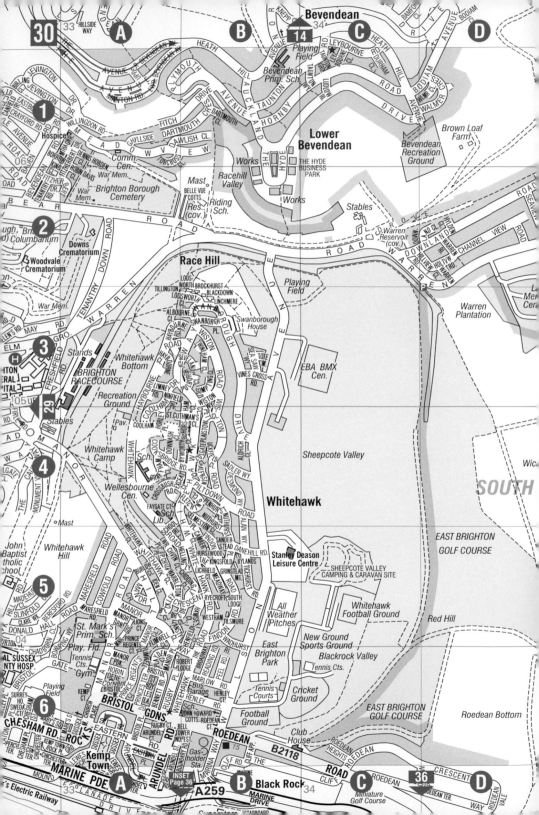

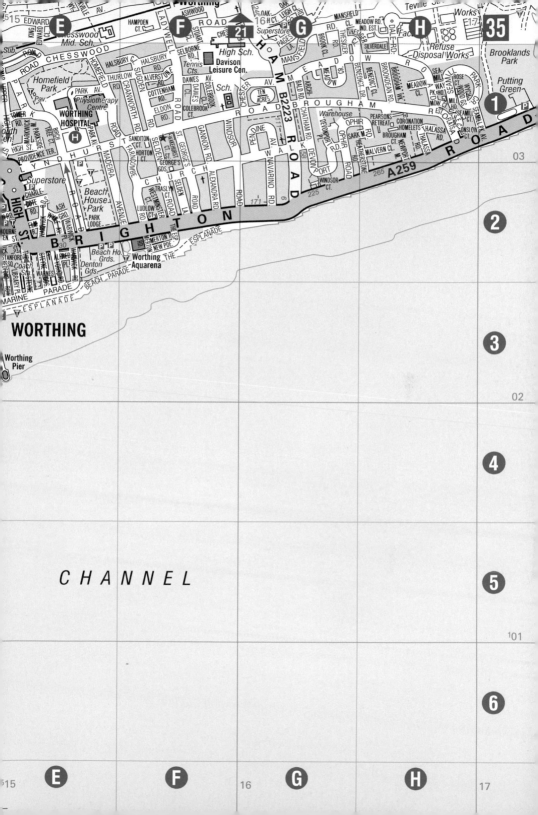

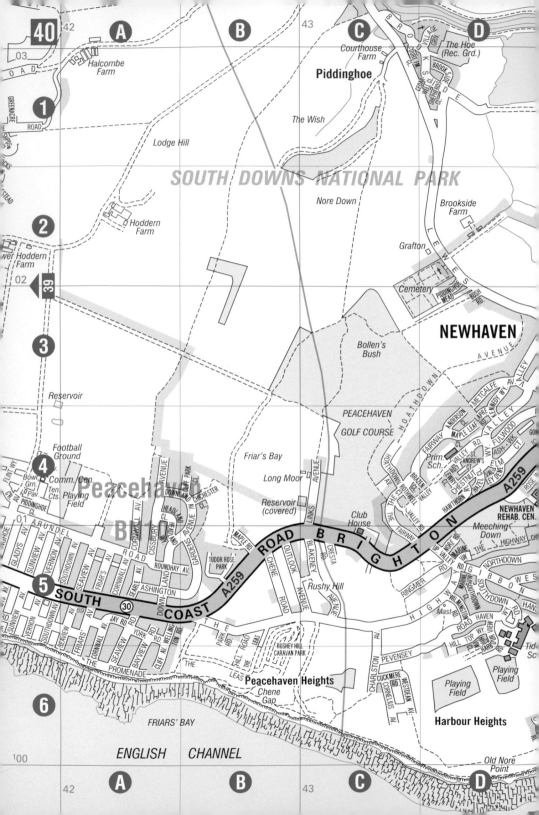

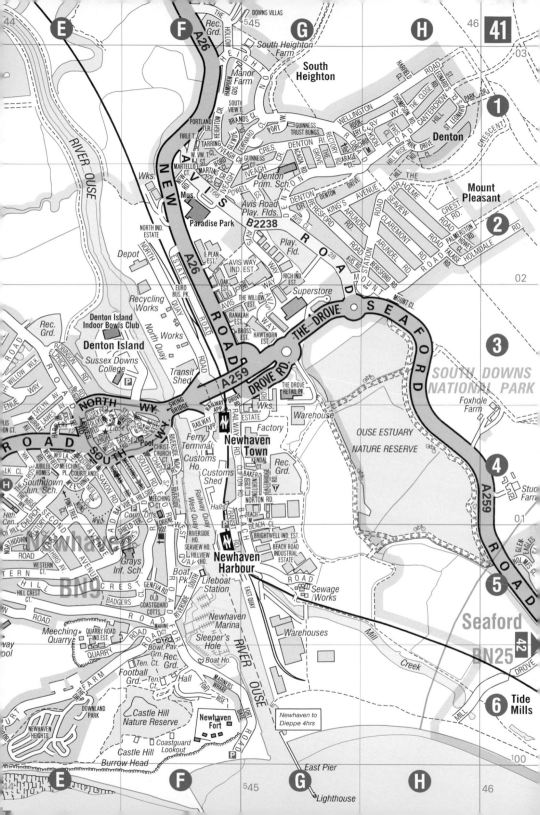

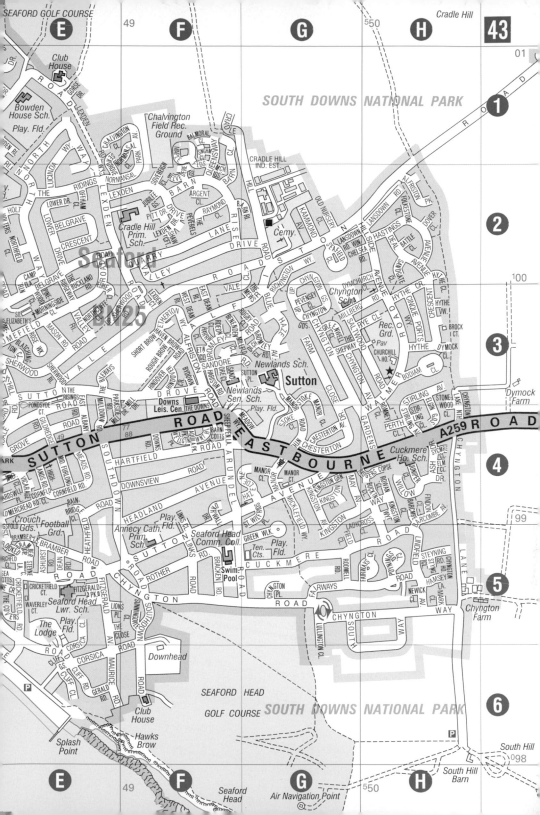

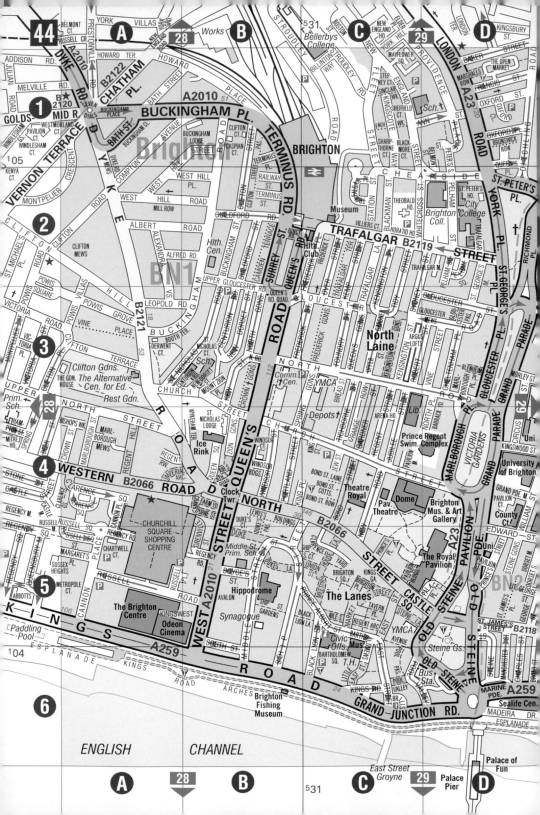

INDEX

Including Streets, Places & Areas, Hospitals etc., Industrial Estates,
Selected Flats & Walkways, Stations and Selected Places of Interest.

HOW TO USE THIS INDEX

1. Each street name is followed by its Postcode District, then by its Locality abbreviation(s) and then by its map reference;
e.g. **Ainsworth Av.** BN2: O'dean . . . .1D **36** is in the BN2 Postcode District and the Ovingdean Locality and is to be found in square 1D on page **36**.
The page number is shown in bold type.

2. A strict alphabetical order is followed in which Av., Rd., St., etc. (though abbreviated) are read in full and as part of the street name;
e.g. **Ash Ct.** appears after **Ashcombe Hollow** but before **Ashcroft**

3. Streets and a selection of flats and walkways that cannot be shown on the mapping, appear in the index with the thoroughfare to which they are connected
shown in brackets; e.g. **Abergavenny Ho.** BN3: Hove . . . .4B **28** (off Holland Rd.)

4. Addresses that are in more than one part are referred to as not continuous.

5. Places and areas are shown in the index in BLUE TYPE and the map reference is to the actual map square in which the town centre or area is located and
not to the place name shown on the map; e.g. **BRAMBER** 4E **5**

6. An example of a selected place of interest is **Barbican House Mus.** 4E **17**

7. An example of a station is **Aldrington Station (Rail)** . . . .2G **27**, also included is **Park & Ride**.
e.g. **Withdean (Park & Ride)** 4B **12**

8. An example of a Hospital or Hospice is **ACRE DAY HOSPITAL** 3C **34**

9. Map references for entries that appear on large scale page **44** are shown first, with small scale map references shown in brackets;
e.g. **Abbotts** BN1: Brig 5A **44** (5C **28**)

GENERAL ABBREVIATIONS

App. : Approach	Cotts. : Cottages	Ho. : House	Quad. : Quadrant
Arc. : Arcade	Ct. : Court	Ind. : Industrial	Ri. : Rise
Av. : Avenue	Cres. : Crescent	Info. : Information	Rd. : Road
Blvd. : Boulevard	Cft. : Croft	Junc. : Junction	Rdbt. : Roundabout
Bri. : Bridge	Dr. : Drive	La. : Lane	Shop. : Shopping
B'way. : Broadway	E. : East	Lit. : Little	Sth. : South
Bldgs. : Buildings	Ent. : Enterprise	Lwr. : Lower	Sq. : Square
Bungs. : Bungalows	Est. : Estate	Mnr. : Manor	St. : Street
Bus. : Business	Fld. : Field	Mans. : Mansions	Ter. : Terrace
Cvn. : Caravan	Flds. : Fields	Mdw. : Meadow	Twr. : Tower
C'way. : Causeway	Gdn. : Garden	M. : Mews	Trad. : Trading
Cen. : Centre	Gdns. : Gardens	Mt. : Mount	Up. : Upper
Cir. : Circus	Gth. : Garth	Mus. : Museum	Va. : Vale
Cl. : Close	Ga. : Gate	Nth. : North	Vw. : View
Coll. : College	Gt. : Great	Pde. : Parade	Vs. : Villas
Comn. : Common	Grn. : Green	Pk. : Park	Wlk. : Walk
Cnr. : Corner	Gro. : Grove	Pas. : Passage	W. : West
Cott. : Cottage	Hgts. : Heights	Pl. : Place	Yd. : Yard

LOCALITY ABBREVIATIONS

Ang : Angmering	Gor S : Goring-by-Sea	Peace : Peacehaven	S Lan : South Lancing
Bramb : Bramber	High S : High Salvington	Pidd : Piddinghoe	S'wick : Southwick
Brig : Brighton	Hove : Hove	Port : Portslade	Stan : Stanmer
Broad : Broadwater	King G : Kingston Gorse	Rott : Rottingdean	Stey : Steyning
Char D : Charman Dean	King L : Kingston near Lewes	Salt : Saltdean	Tel C : Telscombe Cliffs
Clap : Clapham	Lan : Lancing	Salv : Salvington	Up B : Upper Beeding
Durr : Durrington	Lew : Lewes	Sea : Seaford	W Tar : West Tarring
Falm : Falmer	New : Newhaven	Shor B : Shoreham Beach	Wis : Wiston
Fer : Ferring	N Lan : North Lancing	Shor S : Shoreham-by-Sea	W'dean : Woodingdean
Fin : Findon	Off : Offham	S Dole : Small Dole	Wor : Worthing
Fin V : Findon Valley	O'dean : Ovingdean	Somp : Sompting	
Glyn : Glynde	Pat : Patching	S Heig : South Heighton	

A

Abbey Cl. BN10: Peace 3G **39**
  BN15: S Lan 4F **23**
Abbey Rd. BN2: Brig 6H **29**
  BN11: Wor 3B **34**
  BN15: Somp 3A **22**
  BN44: Stey 2D **4**
Abbotsbury Cl. BN2: Salt 3H **37**
Abbots Way BN15: Lan 4D **22**
Abbotts BN1: Brig 5A **44** (5C **28**)
Abbotts Cl. BN11: Wor 2D **34**
Abbotts Vw. BN15: Somp 2A **22**
A'Becket Ct. BN13: Durr 4G **19**
Aberdeen Rd. BN2: Brig 2G **29**
Abergavenny Ho. BN3: Hove 4B **28**
            (off Holland Rd.)
Abergavenny Rd. BN7: Lew 4D **16**
Abingdon Wlk. BN13: Durr 5F **19**
          (off Middle Tyne)
Abinger Ct. BN41: Port 2B **26**
          (off Abinger Rd.)

Abinger Pl. BN7: Lew 4E **17**
Abinger Rd. BN2: W'dean 4G **31**
  BN41: Port 2B **26**
Acacia Av. BN3: Hove 1F **27**
  BN13: Durr 3H **19**
Acacia Ct. BN1: Brig 6D **12**
Acacia Rd. BN9: New 1G **41**
Acre Cl., The BN11: Wor 3B **34**
ACRE DAY HOSPITAL 3C **34**
Adams Cl. BN1: Brig 6F **13**
Addison Cl. BN15: Lan 4C **22**
Addison Rd.
  BN3: Hove 1A **44** (3C **28**)
Adelaide Cl. BN13: Durr 3E **19**
  BN25: Sea 2D **42**
Adelaide Cres. BN3: Hove 5A **28**
Adelaide Mans. BN3: Hove 5A **28**
Adelaide Sq. BN43: Shor S 3D **24**
Admiral Ct. BN15: Lan 6B **22**
Admirals Wlk. BN43: Shor B . .4B **24**
  BN43: Shor S 1A **24**
Adur Cl. BN15: S Lan 5G **23**

Adur Ct. BN43: Shor S 2E **25**
Adur Dr. BN43: Shor S 3C **24**
Adur Indoor Bowls Cen. 3H **25**
Adur Outdoor Activities Cen. . . .3A **24**
Adur Rd. BN43: Shor S 2A **24**
Adur Valley Ct. BN44: Up B 4G **5**
           (off Towers Rd.)
Adur Vw. BN44: Up B 4F **5**
Adversane Rd. BN14: Wor 5B **20**
Aglaia Rd. BN11: Wor 3H **33**
Agnes St. BN2: Brig 3G **29**
Ainsdale Cl. BN13: Durr 4F **19**
Ainsdale Rd. BN13: Durr 4F **19**
Ainsworth Av. BN2: O'dean 1D **36**
Ainsworth Cl. BN2: O'dean 6F **31**
Ainsworth Ho. BN2: Brig 3G **29**
Airedale Rd. BN11: Wor 2B **34**
Airlie Ho. BN3: Hove 4A **28**
          (off Grand Av.)
Air St. BN1: Brig 4B **44** (5D **28**)
Alandale Rd. BN15: Somp 2A **22**
Alan Way BN2: Brig 4B **30**
Albany Cl. BN11: Wor 3A **34**

Albany M. BN3: Hove 4H **27**
Albany Rd. BN25: Sea 4B **42**
Albany Towers BN3: Hove 5H **27**
        (off St Catherine's Ter.)
Albany Vs. BN3: Hove 5H **27**
          (off Marine Pde.)
Albemarle, The BN2: Brig 6D **44**
Albemarle Ho. BN11: Wor 2A **34**
         (off Southview Dr.)
Albemarle Mans.
    BN3: Hove 5A **28**
         (off Medina Ter.)
Alberta Rd. BN13: Durr 4F **19**
Alberta Wlk. BN13: Durr 4F **19**
Albert Mans. BN3: Hove 4A **28**
         (off Church Rd.)
Albert M. BN3: Hove 4A **28**
Albert Rd.
  BN1: Brig 2A **44** (4D **28**)
  BN42: S'wick 3F **25**
Albion Ct. BN2: Brig 5F **29**
          (off George St.)
Albion Hill BN2: Brig 4F **29**

Albion Ho.—Bayview Rd.

Albion Ho. *BN2: Brig* . . . *4F 29*
(off Albion St.)
BN42: S'wick . . . 3H 25
Albion St. BN2: Brig . . . 4F 29
BN7: Lew . . . 4F 17
BN41: Port . . . 3B 26
BN42: S'wick . . . 4F 25
Albourne Cl. BN2: Brig . . . 3A 30
Alces Pl. BN25: Sea . . . 2D 42
Alder Cl. BN13: Durr . . . 5E 19
Alderney Rd. BN12: Fer . . . 4B 32
Aldrich Cl. BN2: Brig . . . 4B 30
ALDRINGTON . . . 3F 27
Aldrington Av. BN3: Hove . . . 2G 27
Aldrington Cl. BN3: Hove . . . 3D 26
ALDRINGTON HOUSE . . . **3F 27**
Aldrington Pl. BN3: Hove . . . 2D 26
Aldrington Station (Rail) . . . **2G 27**
Aldsworth Av. BN12: Gor S . . . 2D 32
Aldsworth Ct. BN12: Gor S . . . 2D 32
Aldsworth Pde. BN12: Gor S . . . 2D 32
Aldwick Cres. BN14: Fin V . . . 1A 20
Alexander Ter. *BN11: Wor* . . . *2D 34*
(off Liverpool Gdns.)
Alexandra Cl. BN25: Sea . . . 2D 42
Alexandra Ct. BN3: Hove . . . 6F 11
BN12: Gor S . . . 1E 33
Alexandra Rd. BN11: Wor . . . 2F 35
BN15: S Lan . . . 5D 22
Alexandra Vs.
BN1: Brig . . . 2A 44 (4D 28)
Alfa Ct. BN10: Tel C . . . 5E 39
Alford Cl. BN14: Salv . . . 3A 20
Alfred Davey Ct. *BN1: Brig* . . . *3C 44*
(off Tichbourne St.)
Alfred Pl. BN11: Wor . . . 2E 35
Alfred Rd. BN1: Brig . . . 2A 44 (4D 28)
Alfriston Cl. BN2: Brig . . . 4B 30
BN14: Wor . . . 5B 20
Alfriston Ho. *BN14: Broad* . . . *5D 20*
(off Broadwater St. E.)
Alfriston Pk. BN25: Sea . . . 2H 43
Alfriston Rd. BN14: Wor . . . 5B 20
BN25: Sea . . . 3F 43
Alice Cl. BN3: Hove . . . 5B 28
Alice St. BN3: Hove . . . 5B 28
Alinora Av. BN12: Gor S . . . 2F 33
Alinora Cl. BN12: Gor S . . . 2F 33
Alinora Cres. BN12: Gor S . . . 4E 33
Alinora Dr. BN12: Gor S . . . 3E 33
Allendale Av. BN14: Fin V . . . 1A 20
Allington Rd. BN14: Broad . . . 3E 21
All Saints Arts & Youth Cen. . . . ***4F 17***
(off Friar's Wlk.)
Alma St. BN15: S Lan . . . 6C 22
Almond Av. BN43: Shor S . . . 2G 23
Alpine Rd. BN3: Hove . . . 2F 27
Alston Way BN13: Durr . . . 5F 19
Alverstone Rd. BN11: Wor . . . 1F 35
Ambassadors, The *BN3: Hove* . . . *4A 28*
(off Wilbury Rd.)
Amber Ct. BN3: Hove . . . 3B 28
(Bell Mead)
BN3: Hove . . . 4A 28
(Salisbury Rd.)
Amberley Cl. BN3: Hove . . . 5E 11
BN43: Shor S . . . 1B 24
Amberley Ct. BN11: Wor . . . 2H 33
BN15: S Lan . . . 4D 22
Amberley Dr. BN3: Hove . . . 6E 11
BN12: Gor S . . . 4C 32
Amberley Lodge *BN2: Brig* . . . *4B 30*
(off Whitehawk Way)
Ambleside Av. BN10: Tel C . . . 5E 39
Ambleside Ct. BN10: Tel C . . . 5E 39
Ambleside Rd. BN15: Somp . . . 4A 22
Ambrose Pl. BN11: Wor . . . 2D 34
Amelia Ct. BN11: Wor . . . 2D 34
Amelia Cres. *BN11: Wor* . . . *2C 34*
(off Amelia Rd.)
Amelia Rd. BN11: Wor . . . 2C 34
Amesbury Cres. BN3: Hove . . . 3E 27
AMF Bowling
Worthing . . . **3D 34**
Amherst Cres. BN3: Hove . . . 2F 27
Amhurst Rd. BN10: Tel C . . . 5D 38
Anchor Cl. BN43: Shor B . . . 4C 24
Anchor Ct. BN12: Gor S . . . 3G 33
Ancren Cl. BN12: Fer . . . 6B 18
Anderson Cl. BN9: New . . . 4D 40
Andrew Cl. BN44: Stey . . . 4C 4
Anglesea St. BN11: Wor . . . 1C 34
Angmering Ct. *BN1: Brig* . . . *3B 14*
(off Newick Rd.)
Angola Rd. BN14: Broad . . . 6F 21
Angus Rd. BN12: Gor S . . . 2G 33
Anne of Cleves House . . . **5E 17**
Annes Path BN7: Lew . . . 6E 17
Annington Commercial Cen.
BN44: Bramb . . . 6D 4
Annington Gdns.
BN43: Shor S . . . 1B 24
Annington Rd.
BN44: Bramb . . . 5D 4
Ann St. BN1: Brig . . . 1D 44 (3E 29)
BN11: Wor . . . 2D 34
Annweir Av. BN15: Lan . . . 4B 22
Anscombe Cl. BN11: Wor . . . 3H 33
Anscombe Rd. BN11: Wor . . . 3H 33
Ansisters Rd. BN12: Fer . . . 3A 32
Anson Ct. BN12: Gor S . . . 6E 19
Anson Ho. BN10: Peace . . . 3G 39
Anson Rd. BN12: Gor S . . . 6E 19
Ansty Cl. BN2: Brig . . . 5A 30
Antioch St. BN7: Lew . . . 5E 17
Antony Cl. BN25: Sea . . . 1A 42
Anvil Cl. BN41: Port . . . 6B 10
Anzac Cl. BN10: Peace . . . 3G 39
Appledore Rd. BN2: Brig . . . 4B 14
Applesham Av. BN3: Hove . . . 6E 11
Applesham Ct. BN15: Lan . . . 6C 22
Applesham Way
BN41: Port . . . 1A 26
Approach, The BN1: Brig . . . 5C 12
April Cl. BN12: Fer . . . 4A 32
Apsley Way BN13: Durr . . . 5D 18
Aqua Ct. BN10: Tel C . . . 5D 38
Aquarius Cl. BN10: Peace . . . 6G 39
Aquila Pk. BN25: Sea . . . 4F 43
Archibald Rd. BN11: Wor . . . 1G 35
Ardale Cl. BN11: Wor . . . 2H 33
Ardingly Ct. *BN2: Brig* . . . *5F 29*
(off High St.)
Ardingly Dr. BN12: Gor S . . . 1D 32
Ardingly Rd. BN2: Salt . . . 4B 38
Ardingly St. BN2: Brig . . . 5F 29
Ardsheal Cl. BN14: Broad . . . 4C 20
Ardsheal Rd. BN14: Broad . . . 4C 20
Arena Ho. BN1: Brig . . . 4C 44
Argent Cl. BN25: Sea . . . 2F 43
Argus Lofts BN1: Brig . . . 3C 44
Argyle Rd. BN1: Brig . . . 2D 28
Argyle Vs. *BN1: Brig* . . . *2D 28*
(off Argyle Rd.)
Ariadne Rd. BN11: Wor . . . 3B 34
Ariel Ct. BN15: Lan . . . 6B 22
Arlington Av. BN12: Gor S . . . 3D 32
Arlington Cl. BN12: Gor S . . . 3D 32
Arlington Cres. BN1: Brig . . . 3A 14
Arlington Gdns. BN2: Salt . . . 1B 38
Arlington M. *BN2: Brig* . . . *6H 29*
(off Eastern Rd.)
Arnold St. BN2: Brig . . . 3G 29
Arnside Cl. BN15: Somp . . . 5A 22
Arthur St. BN3: Hove . . . 2G 27
Arts Rd. BN1: Falm . . . 1D 14
Arun Cl. BN13: Durr . . . 3F 19
BN15: Somp . . . 3A 22
Arun Ct. BN43: Shor S . . . 2E 25
Arun Cres. BN13: Durr . . . 3E 19
Arundel Cl. BN43: Shor S . . . 2E 25
Arundel Ct. *BN1: Brig* . . . *3A 12*
(off Mill Ri.)
BN2: Brig . . . 4A 36
BN11: Wor . . . 2H 33
BN12: Fer . . . 4B 32
BN43: Shor S . . . 2E 25
Arundel Dr. E. BN2: Salt . . . 3A 38
Arundel Dr. W. BN2: Salt . . . 3H 37
Arundel Grn. BN7: Lew . . . 3D 16
Arundel M. *BN2: Brig* . . . *4A 36*
(off Arundel Pl.)
Arundel Pl. BN2: Brig . . . 4A 36
Arundel Rd. BN2: Brig . . . 5A 36
BN9: New . . . 2G 41
BN10: Peace . . . 5F 39
(not continuous)
BN13: Clap, High S, Pat . . . 2A 18
BN25: Sea . . . 4F 43
Arundel Rd. W. BN10: Peace . . . 4E 39
Arundel St. BN2: Brig . . . 5A 36
Arundel Ter. BN2: Brig . . . 5A 36
Ashacre La. BN13: Salv . . . 3H 19
Ashacre M. BN13: Salv . . . 3H 19
Ashacre Way BN13: Salv . . . 3H 19
Ashburnham Cl. BN1: Brig . . . 3H 13
BN13: Durr . . . 5D 18
Ashburnham Dr. BN1: Brig . . . 2H 13
Ash Cl. BN3: Hove . . . 5A 12
BN14: Fin . . . 2C 6
Ashcombe Hollow
BN7: King L, Lew . . . 6A 16
Ash Ct. BN42: S'wick . . . 1H 25
Ashcroft BN43: Shor S . . . 3F 25
Ashcroft Cl. BN43: Shor S . . . 3F 25
Ashdown BN3: Hove . . . 4A 28
Ashdown Av. BN2: Salt . . . 3H 37
Ashdown Rd. BN2: Brig . . . 2F 29
BN11: Wor . . . 1D 34
Ash Dr. BN25: Sea . . . 4H 43
Ashfold Av. BN14: Fin V . . . 1A 20
Ashford Rd. BN1: Brig . . . 6E 13
Ash Gro. BN11: Wor . . . 2E 35
Ashington Ct. *BN2: Brig* . . . *4B 30*
(off Whitehawk Way)
BN14: Broad . . . *5D 20*
(off Broadway St. E.)
Ashington Gdns. BN10: Peace . . . 5A 40
Ashleigh Glegg Ho.
BN25: Sea . . . *3C 42*
(off Grosvenor Rd.)
Ashley Cl. BN1: Brig . . . 1C 12
Ashley Ho. BN3: Hove . . . 5H 27
Ashlings Way BN3: Hove . . . 6E 11
BN43: Shor S . . . 1D 24
Ashmore Cl. BN10: Peace . . . 2H 39
Ashton Lodge *BN2: Brig* . . . *4F 29*
(off Ashton Ri.)
Ashton Ri. BN2: Brig . . . 4F 29
Ashurst Av. BN2: Salt . . . 4C 38
Ashurst Cl. BN12: Gor S . . . 3D 32
Ashurst Dr. BN12: Gor S . . . 3D 32
Ashurst Rd. BN2: Brig . . . 3B 14
BN25: Sea . . . 5E 43
Ash Wlk. BN9: New . . . 4D 40
Ashwood Cl. BN11: Wor . . . 6F 21
Aspen Ct. BN15: Lan . . . 6A 22
Aston Ho. BN43: Shor S . . . 2A 24
Astra Ho. *BN1: Brig* . . . *5C 28*
(off King's Rd.)
Athelstan Rd. BN14: W Tar . . . 6A 20
Athenaeum, The BN3: Hove . . . 4A 28
Atlantic Ct. BN43: Shor B . . . 4B 24
Atlingworth Ct. *BN2: Brig* . . . *6F 29*
(off Atlingworth St.)
Atlingworth St. BN2: Brig . . . 6F 29
Atrium Ho. BN1: Brig . . . 3C 44
Attree Ct. BN2: Brig . . . 4G 29
Attree Dr. BN2: Brig . . . 4G 29
Auckland Dr. BN2: Brig . . . 1B 30
Audrey Cl. BN1: Brig . . . 3C 12
BN25: Sea . . . 2C 42
Augusta Ho. BN11: Wor . . . 3D 34
Augusta Pl. BN11: Wor . . . 3D 34
Avalon BN1: Brig . . . 5B 44 (5D 28)
Avalon Way BN13: Durr . . . 4F 19
Avenue BN1: Brig . . . 5C 44
Avenue, The BN2: Brig . . . 6H 13
BN7: Lew . . . 4D 16
BN12: Gor S . . . 6E 19
BN43: Shor S . . . 1A 24
Avenue Ct. *BN3: Hove* . . . *4A 28*
(off Palmeira Av.)
Avery Cl. BN41: Port . . . 4H 9
Avila Ho. *BN11: Wor* . . . *2C 34*
(off Gratwicke Rd.)
Avis Cl. BN9: New . . . 2G 41
Avis Pde. Shops *BN9: New* . . . *2G 41*
(off Avis Rd.)
Avis Rd. BN9: New . . . 2F 41
(not continuous)
Avis Way BN9: New . . . 2G 41
Avis Way Ind. Est. BN9: New . . . 2F 41
Avon Cl. BN15: Somp . . . 4H 21
Avon Ct. *BN2: Brig* . . . *5F 29*
(off Mt. Pleasant)
BN15: Somp . . . 4H 21
Avondale Cl. BN12: Gor S . . . 1F 33
Avondale Ct. *BN25: Sea* . . . *4D 42*
(off Avondale Rd.)
Avondale Rd. BN3: Hove . . . 3B 28
BN25: Sea . . . 4D 42
Aylesbury BN3: Hove . . . 4C 28
Aymer Ho. BN3: Hove . . . 4G 27
Aymer Rd. BN3: Hove . . . 4G 27
Aynsley Ct. BN3: Hove . . . 2A 28

B

Baden Rd. BN2: Brig . . . 1H 29
Badger Cl. BN41: Port . . . 6B 10
Badgers Cl. BN9: New . . . 5E 41
Badgers Copse BN25: Sea . . . 4H 43
Badgers Fld. BN10: Peace . . . 3G 39
Badger Way BN1: Brig . . . 2A 14
Bainbridge Cl. BN25: Sea . . . 4E 43
Bakers Ct. BN13: Durr . . . 3G 19
Baker St. BN1: Brig . . . 1D 44 (3E 29)
BN9: New . . . 4G 41
Bakery M. BN2: Brig . . . 1G 29
Balcombe Av. BN14: Wor . . . 5C 20
Balcombe Ct. BN10: Peace . . . 4G 39
BN11: Wor . . . 3B 34
Balcombe Rd. BN10: Peace . . . 4F 39
Balfour Rd. BN1: Brig . . . 6D 12
Balfour Vs. BN1: Brig . . . 6E 13
Ball Tree Cft. BN15: Somp . . . 3A 22
Balmoral Cl. BN25: Sea . . . 1F 43
Balmoral Ct. BN3: Hove . . . 5G 11
BN11: Wor . . . 2A 34
Balsdean Rd. BN2: W'dean . . . 1F 31
Baltimore Ct. BN3: Hove . . . 3A 28
Bamford Cl. BN2: Brig . . . 6C 14
Bampfield St. BN41: Port . . . 2B 26
Bank Pas. *BN11: Wor* . . . *2D 34*
(off Liverpool Rd.)
BN44: Stey . . . 3C 4
Bankside BN1: Brig . . . 3A 12
Bankside Ct. *BN1: Brig* . . . *3A 12*
(off Bankside)
Bannings Va. BN2: Salt . . . 4B 38
Banstead Cl. BN12: Gor S . . . 4E 33
Baranscraig Av. BN1: Brig . . . 1E 13
Barbary La. BN12: Fer . . . 3A 32
Barber Ct. *BN7: Lew* . . . *5D 16*
(off St Pancras Rd.)
Barbican House Mus. . . . **4E 17**
Barclay Ho. BN2: Brig . . . 3F 29
Barcombe Av. BN25: Sea . . . 4H 43
Barcombe Cl. BN25: Sea . . . 4H 43
Barcombe Pl. BN1: Brig . . . 3B 14
Barcombe Rd. BN1: Brig . . . 4A 14
Barfield Pk. BN15: Lan . . . 4D 22
Barley Cl. BN10: Tel C . . . 2F 39
Barlow Collection, The . . . **1C 14**
Barn Cl. BN13: Durr . . . 3H 19
BN25: Sea . . . 2F 43
Barn Cotts. BN25: Sea . . . 4F 43
Barnes Rd. BN41: Port . . . 2B 26
Barnett Rd. BN1: Brig . . . 6F 13
Barnet Way BN3: Hove . . . 5E 11
BN13: Durr . . . 5F 19
Barnfield Gdns. BN2: Brig . . . 4G 29
Barn Hatch Cl. BN7: Lew . . . 5C 16
Barn Ho., The BN25: Sea . . . 2D 42
Barn Ri. BN1: Brig . . . 3B 12
BN25: Sea . . . 2F 43
Barn Rd. BN7: Lew . . . 2G 17
Barn Theatre, The . . . **3G 25**
Barons Cl. BN25: Sea . . . 2B 42
Barons Ct. BN11: Wor . . . 1C 34
Barons Down Rd. BN7: Lew . . . 5C 16
Barons Wlk. BN7: Lew . . . 5C 16
Barrack Yd. BN1: Brig . . . 4D 44
Barrhill Av. BN1: Brig . . . 1D 12
Barrington Cl. BN12: Gor S . . . 2E 33
Barrington Rd. BN12: Gor S . . . 2E 33
(not continuous)
Barrow Cl. BN1: Brig . . . 6G 13
Barrowfield Cl. BN3: Hove . . . 5A 12
Barrowfield Dr. BN3: Hove . . . 6A 12
Barrowfield Lodge BN3: Hove . . . 6A 12
Barrow Hill BN1: Brig . . . 6G 13
Barry Wlk. BN2: Brig . . . 4G 29
Bartholomews
BN1: Brig . . . 5C 44 (5E 29)
(not continuous)
Bartholomew Sq. BN1: Brig . . . 6C 44
Bartletts Cotts. *BN14: Broad* . . . *5D 20*
(off Broadwater St. E.)
Barton Cl. BN13: W Tar . . . 5A 20
Bashfords La. BN14: Broad . . . 6D 20
Basin Rd. Nth. BN41: Port . . . 4C 26
Basin Rd. Sth. BN41: Port . . . 4G 25
BN42: Port, S'wick . . . 4G 25
Batemans Cl. BN13: Durr . . . 5D 18
Batemans Rd. BN2: W'dean . . . 3G 31
Bates Rd. BN1: Brig . . . 6D 12
Bath Ct. *BN3: Hove* . . . *5H 27*
(off King's Esplanade)
Bath Pl. BN11: Wor . . . 3D 34
Bath Rd. BN11: Wor . . . 3A 34
Bath St. BN1: Brig . . . 1A 44 (3D 28)
Battle Cl. BN25: Sea . . . 2H 43
Bavant Rd. BN1: Brig . . . 6C 12
Baxter Rd. BN7: Lew . . . 3D 16
Baxter St. BN2: Brig . . . 3G 29
Bay Tree Cl. BN43: Shor S . . . 1E 25
Bayview Rd. BN10: Peace . . . 6A 40

Bay Vue Rd.—Brighton

Bay Vue Rd. BN9: New 4E **41**
Baywood Gdns. BN2: W'dean ... 2E **31**
Bazehill Rd. BN2: Rott 2F **37**
Beach Cl. BN9: New 5G **41**
BN25: Sea 4C **42**
Beach Cotts. BN25: Sea 3B **42**
Beach Ct. BN43: Shor B 4C **24**
Beachcroft Pl. BN15: S Lan 6C **22**
Beach Grn. BN43: Shor B 4H **23**
Beach House Pk. **2E 35**
Beach M. BN9: New 4G **41**
Beach Pde. BN11: Wor 3E **35**
Beach Rd. BN9: New 4G **41**
BN43: Shor B 5A **24**
Beach Rd. Ind. Est. BN9: New ... 5G **41**
Beachside Cl. BN12: Gor S 3G **33**
Beacon Cl. BN1: Brig 6E **13**
BN25: Sea 2C **42**
Beacon Ct. BN2: O'dean 6F **31**
Beacon Dr. BN25: Sea 2C **42**
Beacon Hill BN2: O'dean 1E **37**
Beacon Ho. *BN3: Hove 3D **26***
(off Erroll Rd.)
Beacon Mill **3F 37**
Beacon Rd. BN25: Sea 3C **42**
(Hawth Way)
BN25: Sea 3C **42**
(Kingsway)
Beaconsfield Pde. *BN1: Brig 2D **28***
(off Beaconsfield Rd.)
Beaconsfield Rd. BN1: Brig 2E **29**
BN41: Port 2B **26**
Beaconsfield Vs. BN1: Brig 6D **12**
Beaconsville Ct. BN1: Brig 1D **28**
Beal Cres. BN1: Brig 6F **13**
Beame Ct. BN25: Sea 4C **42**
Bear Rd. BN2: Brig 2G **29**
Bear Yd. BN7: Lew 4F **17**
Beatty Av. BN1: Brig 1H **13**
Beaufort Ter. BN2: Brig 4G **29**
Beau Ho. *BN1: Brig 1A **44***
(off Bath St.)
Beaumont Rd. BN14: Broad 5D **20**
Beccles Rd. BN11: Wor 2B **34**
Becket Rd. BN14: Wor 1A **34**
Beckett Way BN7: Lew 2E **17**
Beckley Cl. BN2: Brig 5A **30**
Beckworth Cl. BN13: Durr 5D **18**
Bedford Pl. BN1: Brig 5C **28**
Bedford Row BN11: Wor 2E **35**
Bedford Sq. BN1: Brig 5C **28**
Bedford St. BN2: Brig 6G **29**
Bedford Towers *BN1: Brig 5C **28***
(off King's Rd.)
Beech Cl. BN14: Fin 1C **6**
BN41: Port 5H **9**
Beechers Rd. BN41: Port 5H **9**
Beeches, The BN1: Brig 5B **12**
Beeches Av. BN14: Char D 3D **20**
Beech Gdns. BN14: Wor 6C **20**
Beech Gro. BN2: Brig 5A **14**
BN15: S Lan 5E **23**
Beech Rd. BN14: Fin 1C **6**
Beechwood BN1: Brig 5C **12**
Beechwood Av. BN1: Brig 4D **12**
BN13: Durr 3H **19**
Beechwood Cl. BN1: Brig 4D **12**
Beeding Av. BN3: Hove 5F **11**
Beeding Cl. BN15: Somp 2B **22**
Beeding Ct. *BN1: Brig 3A **12***
(off Mill Ri.)
BN43: Shor S 2D **24**
Beehive Cl. BN12: Fer 3B **32**
Beehive La. BN12: Fer 3A **32**
Bee Rd. BN10: Peace 4G **39**
Belbourne Ct. *BN1: Brig 3C **44***
(off Tichbourne St.)
Belfast St. BN3: Hove 3H **27**
Belgrave Cres. BN25: Sea 2E **43**
Belgrave Pl. BN2: Brig 6H **29**
Belgrave Rd. BN25: Sea 3C **42**
Belgrave St. BN2: Brig 4F **29**
Belle Vue Cotts. BN2: Brig 2B **30**
Belle Vue Ct. BN2: Brig 5H **29**
Bellevue Ct. BN1: Brig 1D **28**
Belle Vue Gdns. BN2: Brig 5G **29**
Bellingham Cres. BN3: Hove 2D **26**
Bell La. BN7: Lew 5D **16**
Bell Mead BN3: Hove 3B **28**
Bell Twr. Ind. Est. BN2: Brig 4B **36**
Bellview Ct. BN13: W Tar 5A **20**
Bellview Rd. BN13: W Tar 5A **20**
Belmaine Ct. BN11: Wor 3C **34**
Belmer Ct. BN11: Wor 3A **34**
Belmont BN1: Brig 3C **28**
Belmont Ct. BN1: Brig 1A **44**
Belmont St.
BN1: Brig 1D **44** (3E **29**)
Belmont Wlk. BN13: Durr 5F **19**
Belsize Cl. BN11: Wor 1A **34**
Belsize Rd. BN11: Wor 1B **34**
Belton Cl. *BN2: Brig 2F **29***
(off Belton Rd.)
Belton Rd. BN2: Brig 2F **29**
Belvedere BN1: Brig 2C **28**
Belvedere Av. BN15: Lan 4B **22**
Belvedere Gdns. BN25: Sea 2F **43**
Belvedere Ter. *BN1: Brig 4C **28***
(off Norfolk Ter.)
Bembridge St. BN2: Brig 2G **29**
Benbow Cl. BN43: Shor B 4B **24**
Benedict Cl. BN11: Wor 1H **35**
Benedict Dr. BN11: Wor 1G **35**
Benenden Cl. BN25: Sea 3F **43**
Benett Av. BN3: Hove 6H **11**
Benett Dr. BN3: Hove 6H **11**
Benfield Cl. BN41: Port 1C **26**
Benfield Ct. BN41: Port 2C **26**
Benfield Cres. BN41: Port 1C **26**
Benfield Way BN41: Port 2C **26**
Bengairn Av. BN1: Brig 1E **13**
Benham Ct. *BN3: Hove 5H **27***
(off King's Esplanade)
Bennett Rd. BN2: Brig 4A **36**
Benson Ct. BN3: Hove 3E **27**
Bentham Rd. BN2: Brig 3G **29**
Berberis Ct. BN43: Shor S 1D **24**
Beresford Ct. BN3: Hove 3B **28**
Beresford Ho. BN10: Peace 3G **39**
Beresford Rd. BN2: Brig 5H **29**
BN9: New 2G **41**
Bergamot Cres. BN43: Shor S ... 1E **25**
Berkeley Ct. *BN3: Hove 3C **28***
(off Davigdor Rd.)
*BN12: Fer 2A **32***
(off Ferringham La.)
Berkeley Row BN7: Lew 5C **16**
Berkeley Sq. BN11: Wor 2A **34**
Berkshire Ct. BN12: Gor S 1D **32**
Bernard Pl. BN2: Brig 3G **29**
Bernard Rd. BN2: Brig 3G **29**
BN11: Wor 3H **33**
Berriedale Av. BN3: Hove 4E **27**
Berriedale Cl. BN15: Somp 3A **22**
Berriedale Dr. BN15: Somp 3A **22**
Berriedale Ho. BN3: Hove 4E **27**
Berry Cl. BN10: Tel C 3E **39**
Berwick Cl. BN25: Sea 3C **42**
Berwick Rd. BN2: Salt 1B **38**
Bessborough Ter. BN15: Lan 6B **22**
Besson Ho. *BN41: Port 3C **26***
(off Gordon Cl.)
BEVENDEAN **1C 30**
Bevendean Av. BN2: Salt 3B **38**
Bevendean Cres. BN2: Brig 6A **14**
Bevendean Rd. BN2: Brig 2H **29**
Beverley Ct. BN3: Hove 3D **26**
BN11: Wor 3B **34**
Beverley Ho. BN15: S Lan 6C **22**
Bexhill Rd. BN2: W'dean 1F **31**
Bigwood Av. BN3: Hove 2B **28**
Billam Ho. *BN2: Brig 4F **29***
(off Belgrave St.)
Billam Ter. *BN2: Brig 4F **29***
(off Belgrave St.)
Billinton Way BN1: Brig 3E **29**
Biology Rd. BN1: Falm 2D **14**
Birch Cl. BN15: Lan 6B **22**
Birch Ct. BN42: S'wick 1A **26**
Birches Cl. BN13: Durr 5E **19**
Birch Gro. Cres. BN1: Brig 3E **13**
Birch Lodge *BN2: Brig 2F **29***
(off Bromley Rd.)
Birch Tree Ct. BN11: Wor 1E **35**
Birdham Pl. BN2: Brig 5A **14**
Birdham Rd. BN2: Brig 5A **14**
Birkdale Cl. BN13: Durr 4F **19**
Birkdale Rd. BN13: Durr 4F **19**
Birling Cl. BN2: Brig 1H **29**
BN25: Sea 3C **42**
Bishops Cl. BN14: W Tar 6A **20**
BN15: Lan 4D **22**
BN25: Sea 3B **42**
Bishops Dr. BN7: Lew 5C **16**
Bishops Rd. BN3: Hove 1A **28**
BISHOPSTONE **1B 42**
Bishopstone Dr. BN2: Salt 2H **37**
Bishopstone Station (Rail) **3A 42**
Bishops Wlk.
BN1: Brig 4A **44** (5D **28**)
Blackdown BN2: Brig 3B **30**
Blackdown Rd. BN13: Durr 3H **19**
Black Lion La.
BN1: Brig 5B **44** (5D **28**)
Black Lion St.
BN1: Brig 6C **44** (6E **29**)
Blackman St.
BN1: Brig 2C **44** (4E **29**)
Blackmore Ct. BN1: Brig 1C **44**
Blackpatch Gro.
BN43: Shor S 1B **24**
BLACK ROCK **5B 36**
Blacksmiths Cres.
BN15: Somp 4H **21**
Blackthorn Cl. BN1: Brig 5B **12**
BN41: Port 6B **10**
Blake Ct. *BN2: Brig 4F **29***
(off Richmond Pl.)
Blakeney Av. BN10: Peace 5C **40**
Blaker St. BN2: Brig 5F **29**
Blatchington Cl. BN25: Sea 3E **43**
Blatchington Hill BN25: Sea 3D **42**
Blatchington Hill Flats
*BN25: Sea 2E **43***
(off Up. Belgrave Rd.)
Blatchington Rd. BN3: Hove 3G **27**
BN25: Sea 4D **42**
Blatchington Rd. Ind. Est.
BN25: Sea 4D **42**
Blenheim Av. BN13: Durr 4G **19**
Blenheim Ct. *BN3: Hove 4G **27***
(off New Chu. Rd.)
BN13: High S 2F **19**
Blenheim Pl.
BN1: Brig 3D **44** (4E **29**)
Blenheim Rd. BN15: Lan 6B **22**
Blessing Lodge *BN43: Shor B ... 4D **24***
(off Britannia Av.)
Bletchley Ct. BN1: Brig 2E **29**
Blois Rd. BN7: Lew 2C **16**
Bloomsbury Pl. BN2: Brig 6G **29**
Bloomsbury St. BN2: Brig 6G **29**
Bluebird Cl. BN43: Shor B 4D **24**
Bluebird Ct. BN3: Hove 4G **27**
Blue Haze Av. BN25: Sea 3G **43**
Blunden's Ride
BN13: Clap .... 6A **6** & 1D **18**
Boardwalk BN2: Brig 5B **36**
Boatyard, The BN2: Brig 1A **36**
Bodiam Av. BN2: Brig 1D **30**
BN12: Gor S 4D **32**
(Amberley Dr.)
BN12: Gor S 2D **32**
(Fernhurst Dr.)
Bodiam Cl. BN2: Brig 6D **14**
BN25: Sea 3H **43**
Bodiham Ho. *BN3: Hove 3B **28***
(off Davigdor Rd.)
Bodmin Cl. BN13: Durr 2F **19**
Bodmin Rd. BN13: Durr 2F **19**
Boiler Ho. Hill BN1: Falm 1D **14**
Bolney Av. BN10: Peace 6G **39**
(not continuous)
Bolney Rd. BN2: Brig 4B **14**
Bolsover Rd. BN3: Hove 3E **27**
BN13: Wor 1G **33**
Bonaventure *BN43: Shor B 4D **24***
(off Britannia Av.)
Bonchurch Rd. BN2: Brig 2G **29**
Bond St. BN1: Brig 4C **44** (5E **29**)
Bond St. Cotts. BN1: Brig 4C **44**
Bond St. Laine BN1: Brig 4C **44**
Bond St. Row BN1: Brig 4C **44**
Booth Mus. of Natural History .. **2C 28**
Borough Gate BN44: Stey 3C **4**
Borough St. BN1: Brig 4C **28**
Borrow King Cl. BN2: Brig 1H **29**
Bostal, The BN44: Up B 5H **5**
Bostal Rd. BN44: Bramb, Stey 6A **4**
Bost Hill BN13: Fin V, High S 6C **6**
Boston St. BN1: Brig 1C **44** (3E **29**)
BOTOLPHS **6F 5**
Botolphs Rd. BN44: Bramb 6E **5**
Boughey Pl. BN7: Lew 2E **17**
Boulevard, The BN13: Wor 5F **19**
Boulevard Ho. BN1: Brig 4C **44**
Boundary, The BN25: Sea 5D **42**
Boundary Cl. BN11: Wor 3B **34**
Boundary Pas. *BN1: Brig 4C **28***
(off Norfolk Rd.)
Boundary Rd. BN2: Brig 5A **36**
BN3: Hove 4C **26**
BN11: Wor 3A **34**
BN15: S Lan 5F **23**
Boundstone Cl. BN15: Lan 3B **22**
Boundstone La.
BN15: Lan, Somp 4A **22**
Bourne Cl. BN13: Durr 4D **18**
Bourne Ct. BN1: Brig 4B **12**
Bowden Ri. BN25: Sea 1D **42**
Bowen Ct. BN3: Hove 4A **28**
Bowline Point BN43: Shor S 3A **24**
Bowlplex
Brighton **5B 36**
Bowmans Cl. BN44: Stey 2C **4**
Bowness Av. BN15: Somp 5A **22**
Bowring Way BN2: Brig 6H **29**
Bowser Ct. BN11: Wor 3B **34**
Boxgrove BN12: Gor S 6D **18**
Boxgrove Cl. BN15: N Lan 2D **22**
Boxgrove Pde. BN12: Gor S 6D **18**
Boyce's St.
BN1: Brig 5B **44** (5D **28**)
Boyles La. BN2: Brig 4A **36**
Brackenbury Cl. BN41: Port 6B **10**
Bracken Rd. BN25: Sea 5F **43**
(not continuous)
Bradford Rd. BN7: Lew 4D **16**
Brading Rd. BN2: Brig 3G **29**
Bradley Ho. BN11: Wor 2B **34**
Braemar Ho. *BN1: Brig 4C **28***
(off Norfolk Rd.)
Braemore Ct. BN3: Hove 4F **27**
Braemore Rd. BN3: Hove 4E **27**
Braeside Av. BN1: Brig 1D **12**
Braeside Cl. BN14: Fin 2C **6**
BRAMBER **4E 5**
Bramber Av. BN3: Hove 5F **11**
BN10: Peace 6G **39**
(not continuous)
Bramber Av. Nth.
BN10: Peace 4G **39**
Bramber Castle (remains of) **4E 5**
Bramber Cl. BN10: Peace 4G **39**
BN15: Somp 2B **22**
BN25: Sea 5E **43**
Bramber Ct. BN3: Hove 3H **27**
BN43: Shor S 2C **24**
Bramber La. BN25: Sea 5E **43**
Bramber Rd. BN14: Broad 3E **21**
BN25: Sea 5E **43**
BN44: Stey 4C **4**
Bramble Cl. BN13: Durr 3F **19**
Bramble Cres. BN13: Durr 2F **19**
Brambledean Rd. BN41: Port ... 3B **26**
Bramble La. BN13: Durr 3F **19**
Bramble Ri. BN1: Brig 3A **12**
Brambletyne Av. BN2: Salt 3B **38**
Bramble Way BN1: Brig 2G **13**
Bramley Cl. BN14: Broad 4D **20**
Bramley Rd. BN14: Broad 4D **20**
Brands Cl. BN9: S Heig 1F **41**
Brangwyn Av. BN1: Brig 2C **12**
Brangwyn Ct. BN1: Brig 3B **12**
Brangwyn Cres. BN1: Brig 2B **12**
Brangwyn Dr. BN1: Brig 2B **12**
Brangwyn Way BN1: Brig 3C **12**
Brasslands Dr. BN41: Port 6H **9**
Braybon Av. BN1: Brig 4D **12**
Braypool La. BN1: Brig 1B **12**
Brazen Cl. BN9: New 4C **40**
Breach Cl. BN44: Stey 2C **4**
Bread St. BN1: Brig 3C **44** (4E **29**)
Brecon Cl. BN13: Durr 3H **19**
Brecon Ct. BN3: Hove 3A **28**
Brede Cl. BN2: Brig 5A **30**
Brendon Rd. BN13: Durr 2G **19**
Brentwood Cl. BN1: Brig 5F **13**
Brentwood Cres. BN1: Brig 5F **13**
Brentwood Rd. BN1: Brig 5F **13**
Bretts Fld. BN10: Peace 2G **39**
Brewer St. BN2: Brig 3F **29**
Briar Cl. BN2: W'dean 2F **31**
Briarcroft Rd. BN2: W'dean 3F **31**
Bricky, The BN10: Peace 4G **39**
Bridge Cl. BN12: Gor S 6E **19**
BN15: S Lan 5C **22**
Bridge Ct. *BN9: New 4F **41***
(off Bridge St.)
Bridge Rd. BN14: Broad 1D **34**
Bridge St. BN9: New 4F **41**
Bridge Way BN43: Shor B 4B **24**
Bridgewick Cl. BN7: Lew 2F **17**
Bridgnorth Cl. BN13: Durr 5D **18**
Bridle Cl. BN44: Up B 4G **5**
Bridle Way BN10: Tel C 3E **39**
Brierley Gdns. BN15: Lan 4D **22**
Brigden St. BN1: Brig 3D **28**
Brighthelm BN1: Falm 1D **14**
BRIGHTON .... **4C 44 (5E 29)**

A-Z Brighton & Worthing 47

Cypress Av.—Eastern Ring Rd.

Cypress Av. BN13: Durr 5E 19
Cypress Cl. BN43: Shor S 1B 24
Cyril Richings Bus. Cen.
BN43: Shor S 3D 24

D

Dacre Rd. BN9: New 4F 41
Dagmar St. BN11: Wor 1D 34
Dairy Farm Flats BN12: Gor S 1C 32
Dale Av. BN1: Brig 3D 12
Dale Cres. BN1: Brig 2D 12
Dale Dr. BN1: Brig 2D 12
Dale Rd. BN7: Lew 5C 16
BN11: Wor 6H 21
Dale Vw. BN3: Hove 6D 10
Dale Vw. Gdns. BN3: Hove 6D 10
Dallington Rd. BN3: Hove 2F 27
Damon Cl. BN10: Peace 5G 39
Dana Lodge BN10: Tel C 5E 39
Dane Cl. BN25: Sea 5C 42
Dane Hgts. BN25: Sea 5D 42
Danehill Rd. BN2: Brig 5B 30
Dane Rd. BN25: Sea 5C 42
Daneswood Ho. *BN11: Wor 2A 34*
(off Southview Dr.)
Daniel Cl. BN15: Lan 3D 22
Dankton Gdns. BN15: Somp 3H 21
Dankton La. BN15: Somp 1H 21
Dannfields Ho. BN25: Sea 4C 42
Danny Sheldon Ho. *BN2: Brig 6G 29*
(off Eastern Rd.)
Darcey Dr. BN1: Brig 2E 13
Dart Cl. BN13: Durr 2F 19
Dartmouth Cl. BN2: Brig 1B 30
Dartmouth Cres. BN2: Brig 1A 30
Darwall Dr. BN25: Sea 4F 43
D'Aubigny Rd. BN2: Brig 2F 29
Davenport Ct. BN11: Wor 2H 33
Davey Dr. BN1: Brig 1F 29
Daveys La. BN7: Lew 3G 17
David Lloyd Leisure
Brighton 5A 36
Worthing 5D 18
Davies Ct. BN11: Wor 3A 34
Davigdor Rd. BN3: Hove 3B 28
Davison Leisure Cen. 1F 35
Dawes Av. BN11: Wor 1F 35
Dawes Cl. BN11: Wor 1F 35
Dawlish Cl. BN2: Brig 1A 30
Dawn Cl. BN44: Up B 5G 5
Dawn Cres. BN44: Up B 5F 5
Dawson Ct. *BN11: Wor 1C 34*
(off Victoria Rd.)
Dawson Ter. BN2: Brig 4G 29
Deacons Dr. BN41: Port 6B 10
Deacons Way BN44: Up B 4F 5
Deacon Trad. Est.
BN14: Broad 5F 21
Deacon Way BN14: Broad 5F 21
Deal Av. BN25: Sea 2H 43
Dean Cl. BN2: Rott 2G 37
BN41: Port 6C 10
Dean Ct. Rd. BN2: Rott 2F 37
Deanery Cl. BN7: Lew 2F 17
Dean Gdns. BN41: Port 6C 10
Dean Rd. BN25: Sea 5E 43
Deans Cl. BN2: W'dean 2G 31
Deans Leisure Cen. 6G 31
Dean St. BN1: Brig 4A 44 (5C 28)
Deanway BN3: Hove 5H 11
Deborah Ter. BN10: Tel C 5E 39
De Braose Way BN44: Bramb 4D 4
Deco Bldg., The *BN2: Brig 1G 29*
(off Coombe Rd.)
De Courcel Rd. BN2: Brig 5A 36
Decoy Rd. BN14: Broad 5F 21
Deerswood Cl. BN13: Durr 5D 18
Deeside, The BN1: Brig 1E 13
De Grey Cl. BN7: Lew 3F 17
Delanair Est. BN7: Lew 3F 17
Delaware Rd. BN7: Lew 5C 16
De La Warr Grn. BN7: Lew 2D 16
Delfryn BN41: Port 5G 9
De Montfort Rd. BN2: Brig 3G 29
BN7: Lew 4D 16
Dene, The BN3: Hove 5D 10
Dene Ct. BN11: Wor 2B 34
Denecroft BN1: Brig 3B 12
Deneside BN1: Brig 3B 12
Dene Va. BN1: Brig 3B 12
Deneway, The BN1: Brig 4B 12
BN15: Somp 4A 22
Denmark M. BN3: Hove 3H 27
Denmark Rd. BN41: Port 3C 26
Denmark Ter. BN1: Brig 4C 28
Denmark Vs. BN3: Hove 3H 27
Dennis Hobden Cl. BN2: Brig 1A 30
DENTON 2G 41
Denton Cl. BN12: Gor S 1D 32
Denton Dr. BN1: Brig 3E 13
BN9: New 2G 41
Denton Gdns. 2E 35
DENTON ISLAND 3E 41
Denton Island Indoor Bowls Club 3E 41
Denton Ri. BN9: New 1G 41
Denton Rd. BN9: New 2G 41
Derby Ct. *BN3: Hove 3C 28*
(off Davigdor Rd.)
Derby Pl. *BN2: Brig 5F 29*
(off Up. Park Pl.)
Derek Av. BN3: Hove 4D 26
Derek Ho. BN3: Hove 3F 27
Derek Rd. BN15: N Lan 2B 22
Dervia Ho. *BN3: Hove 3B 28*
(off Palmeira Av.)
Derwent Cl. BN15: Somp 5A 22
Derwent Ct. BN1: Brig 3A 44
Derwent Dr. BN12: Gor S 5F 19
Desmond Way BN2: Brig 4B 30
Devil's Dyke Rd. BN1: Brig 1E 11
Devonian Cl. BN2: Brig 3F 29
Devonian Ct. *BN2: Brig 3F 29*
(off Park Cres. Pl.)
Devon Lodge *BN2: Brig 5F 29*
(off Carlton Hill)
Devonport Pl. BN11: Wor 1G 35
Devonport Rd. BN11: Wor 1G 35
Devonshire Ct. BN3: Hove 3A 28
Devonshire Lodge BN11: Wor 2H 33
Devonshire Pl. BN2: Brig 5F 29
De Warrenne Rd. BN7: Lew 4D 16
Dewe Rd. BN2: Brig 1G 29
Dewpond, The BN10: Peace 3F 39
Diggers, The BN1: Brig 5F 13
Dinapore Ho. *BN2: Brig 4F 29*
(off John St.)
Dingemans BN44: Stey 1C 4
Ditchling Cl. BN12: Gor S 6D 18
Ditchling Ct. *BN1: Brig 2F 29*
(off Ditchling Rd.)
Ditchling Cres. BN1: Brig 3G 13
Ditchling Gdns. BN1: Brig 1E 29
Ditchling Pl. BN1: Brig 1E 29
Ditchling Ri. BN1: Brig 2E 29
Ditchling Rd.
BN1: Brig 1D 44 (5E 13)
BN1: Brig, Stan 1G 13
Dog La. BN44: Stey 3C 4
Dolphin Ct. *BN3: Hove 4G 27*
(off Hove St.)
Dolphin Ind. Est.
BN43: Shor S 3D 24
Dolphin Lodge BN11: Wor 3A 34
Dolphin M. *BN2: Brig 6D 44*
(off Steine St.)
BN43: Shor S 3C 24
Dolphin Rd. BN43: Shor S 3C 24
Dolphin Way BN43: Shor S 3D 24
Dome Cinema *3E 35*
(off Marine Pde.)
Dominion Bldgs. BN14: Broad 6F 21
Dominion Cl. BN14: Broad 6E 21
Dominion Rd. BN14: Broad 5E 21
Dominion Way BN14: Broad 5F 21
Dominion Way W.
BN14: Broad 5F 21
Donald Hall Rd. BN2: Brig 5H 29
Donkey M. BN3: Hove 5B 28
Donnington Rd. BN2: W'dean 4G 31
Doone End BN12: Fer 4B 32
Dorchester Ct. *BN1: Brig 5C 28*
(off Norfolk Sq.)
Dorchester Gdns. BN11: Wor 2A 34
Dorita Ct. *BN10: Peace 5G 39*
(off Sth. Coast Rd.)
Dorothy Av. BN10: Peace 6G 39
(not continuous)
Dorothy Av. Nth. BN10: Peace 4G 39
Dorothy Rd. BN3: Hove 2D 26
Dorset Ct. BN3: Hove 4F 27
Dorset Gdns. BN2: Brig 5F 29
Dorset M. BN2: Brig 5D 44
Dorset Pl. BN2: Brig 5F 29
BN14: W Tar 5A 20
Dorset Rd. BN7: Lew 5F 17
Dorset St. BN2: Brig 5D 44 (5E 29)
Douglas Av. BN11: Wor 2H 33
Douglas Cl. BN11: Wor 2H 33
Dovecote M. BN15: Somp 2A 22
Dover Cl. BN25: Sea 2H 43
Dover Rd. BN1: Brig 6E 13
BN11: Wor 3A 34
Dower Cl. BN2: O'dean 1D 36
Down, The BN3: Hove 4C 10
Downash Cl. BN2: Brig 4A 30
Downes Ct. *BN43: Shor S 2E 25*
(off Wilmot Rd.)
Downe Wlk. *BN13: Durr 5F 19*
(off East Tyne)
Downford *BN2: Brig 5B 30*
(off Whitehawk Rd.)
Downhill Vw. BN2: W'dean 3G 31
Downland Av. BN10: Peace 4A 40
BN42: S'wick 1F 25
Downland Cl. BN2: W'dean 2C 30
BN14: Fin 2C 6
BN42: S'wick 1F 25
BN44: Up B 4G 5
Downland Ct. BN41: Port 6A 10
Downland Cres. BN3: Hove 5F 11
Downland Dr. BN3: Hove 5F 11
Downland Pk. BN9: New 6E 41
BN44: Bramb 5F 5
Downland Rd. BN2: W'dean 2C 30
BN44: Up B 4G 5
Downlands BN13: High S 6C 6
Downlands Av. BN14: Broad 3D 20
Downlands Bus. Pk.
BN14: Char D 2E 21
Downlands Cl. BN15: Somp 3A 22
Downlands Gdns.
BN14: Broad 3E 21
Downlands Pde. *BN14: Broad 3E 21*
(off Up. Brighton Rd.)
Downlands Retail Pk.
BN14: Char D 3E 21
Downs, The BN25: Sea 4F 43
Downsbrook Trad. Est.
BN14: Broad 4E 21
Downs Cl. BN7: Lew 3C 16
BN15: S Lan 4F 23
Downs Crematorium
BN2: Brig 2A 30
Downscroft BN44: Up B 4G 5
Downside BN1: Brig 3B 12
BN3: Hove 5H 11
BN7: Lew 5C 16
BN43: Shor S 1C 24
Downside Av. BN14: Fin V 5C 6
Downside Cl. BN14: Fin V 5D 6
BN43: Shor S 1B 24
Downs Leisure Cen. 3F 43
Downs Link 5E 5
Downsmead BN15: Somp 2A 22
Downs Rd. BN25: Sea 4F 43
Downs Valley Rd.
BN2: W'dean 2G 31
Downs Vw. BN10: Peace 2H 39
Downsview BN3: Hove 5D 10
Downsview Av. BN2: W'dean 2E 31
Downsview Mnr. BN14: Broad 4C 20
Downsview Rd. BN16: King G 4A 32
BN25: Sea 4F 43
BN41: Port 6A 10
Downs Vs. BN9: S Heig 1G 41
Downs Wlk. BN10: Peace 2G 39
Downsway BN2: W'dean 2F 31
BN42: S'wick 6G 9
BN43: Shor S 1B 24
Down Ter. BN2: Brig 4G 29
Downview Av. BN12: Fer 1A 32
Downview Ct. BN11: Wor 3A 34
Downview Rd. BN11: Wor 1A 34
BN12: Fer 1A 32
BN14: Fin 1C 6
Dragons Health Club
Hove 3E 27
Drake Av. BN12: Gor S 6F 19
Drake Ct. BN25: Sea 5D 42
Drakes Cl. BN15: S Lan 4F 23
Draxmont Way BN1: Brig 5D 12
Draycliff Cl. BN12: Fer 3A 32
Dresden Ho. BN3: Hove 4H 27
Driftway, The BN44: Up B 3G 5
Dripping Pan, The 5F 17
Drive, The BN3: Hove 4A 28
BN9: New 6E 41
BN11: Wor 1H 33
BN15: Lan 6B 22
BN42: S'wick 1G 25
BN43: Shor S 2B 24
Drive Lodge BN3: Hove 3A 28
Driveway, The BN43: Shor S 2B 24
Drove, The BN1: Brig 1B 28
BN1: Falm 2E 15
BN9: New 3G 41
Drove Av. BN2: King L 6F 15
BN7: King L 6F 15
Drove Cres. BN41: Port 6A 10
Drove Retail Pk., The
BN9: New 3G 41
Drove Rd. BN2: W'dean 2C 30
(not continuous)
BN9: New 3F 41
BN41: Port 1A 26
Drovers Cl. BN41: Port 6C 10
Droveway, The BN3: Hove 6G 11
(not continuous)
Drummond Ct. *BN12: Gor S 3F 33*
(off Marine Cres.)
Drummond Rd. BN12: Gor S 3G 33
Duchess Dr. BN25: Sea 1D 42
Dudeney Lodge BN1: Brig 1F 29
Dudley M. *BN3: Hove 5B 28*
(off Brunswick St. W.)
Dudley Rd. BN1: Brig 1F 29
Dudwell Rd. BN2: W'dean 3G 31
Duke of York's Picture House 3E 29
Dukes Cl. BN25: Sea 3C 42
Duke's Ct. BN1: Brig 4B 44
Dukes La. BN1: Brig 5B 44 (5D 28)
BN44: Stey 3C 4
Duke's Mound BN2: Brig 6H 29
Duke's Pas. BN1: Brig 5B 44
Duke St. BN1: Brig 5B 44 (5D 28)
Dukes Yd. BN44: Stey 3C 4
Dulwich Cl. BN25: Sea 3G 43
Dumbrell Ct. *BN7: Lew 5D 16*
(off St Pancras Rd.)
Duncan Ct. BN2: Salt 3A 38
Duncan Ho. *BN10: Peace 3G 39*
(off Collingwood Cl.)
Dunster Cl. BN1: Brig 1F 29
Dunvan Cl. BN7: Lew 2E 17
Dunwich *BN43: Shor B 4D 24*
(off Sea Spray Av.)
Durham Cl. BN2: Brig 1C 30
Durham Ct. BN3: Hove 4H 27
DURRINGTON 3F 19
Durrington Ct. *BN1: Brig 3B 12*
(off Mill Ri.)
Durrington Gdns. BN12: Gor S 1F 33
Durrington Hill BN13: Durr 3F 19
Durrington Ho. BN13: Durr 5F 19
Durrington La. BN13: Durr 3F 19
Durrington-on-Sea Station (Rail) 1G 33
Dyke Cl. BN3: Hove 4H 11
Dyke Railway Trail 1D 10
Dyke Rd. BN1: Brig 6B 12
BN3: Hove 1A 44 (6B 12)
Dyke Rd. Av. BN1: Brig 4H 11
BN3: Hove 4H 11
Dyke Rd. Dr. BN1: Brig 2C 28
Dyke Rd. M. BN1: Brig 1A 44
Dyke Rd. Pl. BN1: Brig 5A 12
Dymchurch Cl. BN25: Sea 2G 43
Dymock Cl. BN25: Sea 3H 43

E

Eagle Ct. *BN2: Brig 2G 29*
(off Lewes Rd.)
Earls Cl. BN25: Sea 2B 42
Earls Gdn. BN7: Lew 4F 17
E. Albany Rd. BN25: Sea 3E 43
East Av. BN12: Gor S 3H 33
Eastbank BN42: S'wick 1H 25
EAST BLATCHINGTON 1D 42
Eastbourne Rd. BN2: Brig 1H 29
BN25: Sea 4G 43
Eastbourne Ter. *BN25: Sea 4F 43*
(off Eastbourne Rd.)
Eastbridge Rd. BN9: New 4G 41
Eastbrook Rd. BN41: Port 3B 26
Eastbrook Way BN41: Port 3A 26
Eastcourt Rd. BN14: Broad 6C 20
E. Dean Ri. BN25: Sea 3F 43
East Dr. BN2: Brig 5G 29
Eastergate Cl. BN12: Gor S 1B 32
Eastergate Rd. BN2: Brig 4B 14
Eastern Av. BN43: Shor S 3C 24
Eastern Cl. BN43: Shor S 3C 24
Eastern Concourse BN2: Brig 2A 36
Eastern Pl. BN2: Brig 4A 36
Eastern Ring Rd. BN1: Falm 1D 14

A-Z Brighton & Worthing 51

Fishersgate—Graham Rd.

FISHERSGATE 3A **26**
Fishersgate Cl. BN41: Port 3A **26**
Fishersgate Station (Rail) 3A **26**
Fishersgate Ter. BN41: Port 3A **26**
Fisher St. BN7: Lew 4F **17**
Fitch Dr. BN2: Brig 1A **30**
Fitness First (For Women)
Brighton 2C **44** (4E **29**)
Fittleworth Cl. BN12: Gor S 6C **18**
Fitzalan Ct. *BN10: Peace 5F 39*
(off Cavell Av.)
Fitzgerald Av. BN25: Sea 5E **43**
Fitzgerald Ho. BN25: Sea 4D **42**
Fitzgerald Pk. BN25: Sea 5E **43**
Fitzgerald Rd. BN7: Lew 2F **17**
Fitzherbert Ct. *BN2: Brig 2H 29*
(off Fitzherbert Dr.)
Fitzherbert Dr. BN2: Brig 2H **29**
Fitzjohn's Rd. BN7: Lew 3C **16**
Fitzroy Rd. BN7: Lew 2D **16**
Five Ways BN1: Brig 6E **13**
Flag Ct. BN3: Hove 5H **27**
Flag Sq. BN43: Shor B 4B **24**
Fleet St. BN1: Brig 1C **44** (3E **29**)
Fletcher Rd. BN14: Broad 5E **21**
Fletchers Cft. BN44: Stey 3C **4**
Fletching Cl. BN2: Brig 4B **30**
Flimwell Cl. BN2: Brig 5A **30**
Flint Cl. BN25: Sea 1D **42**
BN41: Port 6B **10**
Flint Way BN10: Peace 5H **39**
Floral Clock *4A 28*
(off Western Rd.)
Floraldene Ct. BN14: Fin V 1A **20**
Florence Av. BN3: Hove 2D **26**
Florence Ct. *BN1: Brig 6D 12*
(off Gordon Rd.)
Florence Pl. BN1: Brig 1F **29**
Florence Rd. BN1: Brig 2E **29**
Florets, The BN44: Up B 5G **5**
Florida Cl. BN12: Fer 4B **32**
Florida Gdns. BN12: Fer 4B **32**
Florida Rd. BN12: Fer 4B **32**
Florlandia Cl. BN15: Somp 4H **21**
Foamcourt Waye BN12: Fer 3A **32**
Folkestone Cl. BN25: Sea 2H **43**
Folly Fld. BN9: New 4E **41**
Fonthill Rd. BN3: Hove 2H **27**
Fontwell Cl. BN14: Fin V 2A **20**
Fontwell Dr. BN14: Fin V 2A **20**
Foredown Cl. BN41: Port 6B **10**
Foredown Dr. BN41: Port 1B **26**
Foredown Rd. BN41: Port 4A **10**
Foredown Tower Countryside Cen.
. . . .**5B 10**
Forest La. BN13: Clap 2D **18**
Forest Rd. BN1: Brig 3A **14**
BN14: Broad 4D **20**
Forge Cl. BN41: Port 6B **10**
Fort Ga. BN9: New 6G **41**
Fort Haven BN43: Shor B 4E **25**
Fort Ri. BN9: New 6F **41**
Fort Rd. BN9: New 4F **41**
Forward Cl. BN9: S Heig 1G **41**
Fosse, The *BN7: Lew 4F 17*
(off Lancaster St.)
Foster Cl. BN25: Sea 3D **42**
Foster Ct. *BN3: Hove 4C 28*
(off York Av.)
Foundry La. BN7: Lew 4G **17**
Foundry St. BN1: Brig . . .3C **44** (4E **29**)
Foundry Ter. *BN7: Lew 4G 17*
(off Foundry La.)
Fountains Cl. BN1: Brig 6F **13**
Founthill Av. BN2: Salt 3H **37**
Founthill Rd. BN2: Salt 3H **37**
Fourth Av. BN3: Hove 5H **27**
BN14: Char D 3D **20**
BN15: Lan 3C **22**
Fowey Cl. BN43: Shor B 4D **24**
Foxdown Rd. BN2: W'dean 3H **31**
Foxglove Wlk. BN13: Durr 5E **19**
Foxhill BN10: Peace 3F **39**
Foxhunters Rd. BN41: Port 5H **9**
Foxlea BN14: Fin 3C **6**
Foxley La. BN13: High S 2G **19**
Fox Way BN41: Port 5A **10**
Framfield *BN2: Brig 5B 30*
(off Whitehawk Rd.)
Framfield Cl. BN1: Brig 2A **14**
Framnaes BN3: Hove 3D **26**
Frampton Ct. BN12: Gor S 2E **33**
Frampton Pl. BN43: Shor S 2H **23**
Framroze Ct. BN1: Brig 5F **13**
Francis St. BN1: Brig . . .1D **44** (3E **29**)
Francome Ho. BN15: Lan 6A **22**
Franklands Cl. BN14: Fin V 1H **19**
Franklin Rd. BN2: Brig 2G **29**
BN13: Durr 3G **19**
BN41: Port 3C **26**
BN43: Shor S 1E **25**
Franklin St. BN2: Brig 2G **29**
Frant Rd. BN3: Hove 6G **11**
Fraser Ct. BN43: Shor S 2E **25**
Fred Emery Ct. *BN1: Brig 5C 28*
(off Sillwood St.)
Frederick Gdns. BN1: Brig 3C **44**
Frederick Pl.
BN1: Brig 2C **44** (4E **29**)
Frederick St.
BN1: Brig 3B **44** (4E **29**)
Frederick Ter. BN1: Brig 2C **44**
Freehold St. BN43: Shor S 3A **24**
Freehold Ter. BN2: Brig 2F **29**
Freeland Cl. BN25: Sea 1A **42**
Freemans Rd. BN41: Port 2A **26**
Frenchs Ct. *BN25: Sea 5D 42*
(off Steyne Rd.)
Freshbrook Cl. BN15: S Lan 5C **22**
Freshbrook Ct. *BN15: Lan 5C 22*
(off Freshbrook Rd.)
Freshbrook Rd.
BN15: Lan, S Lan 5C **22**
Freshfield Ind. Est.
BN2: Brig 5G **29**
Freshfield Pl. BN2: Brig 5G **29**
Freshfield Rd. BN2: Brig 5G **29**
Freshfields Cl. BN15: Lan 4B **22**
Freshfields Dr. BN15: Lan 4B **22**
Freshfield St. BN2: Brig 4G **29**
Freshfield Way BN2: Brig 5G **29**
Friar Cl. BN1: Brig 4E **13**
Friar Cres. BN1: Brig 4E **13**
Friar Rd. BN1: Brig 4D **12**
Friars Av. BN10: Peace 6A **40**
(not continuous)
Friars M. *BN7: Lew 5F 17*
(off Pinwell Rd.)
Friar's Wlk. BN7: Lew 4F **17**
Friar Wlk. BN1: Brig 4D **12**
BN13: Wor 1H **33**
Frimley Cl. BN2: W'dean 3H **31**
Friston Cl. BN2: Brig 4B **14**
BN25: Sea 3B **42**
Frith Rd. BN3: Hove 2G **27**
Frobisher Cl. BN12: Gor S 6F **19**
Frobisher Ho. BN10: Peace 3G **39**
Frobisher Way BN12: Gor S 6F **19**
Fulbeck Av. BN13: Durr 4D **18**
Fuller Rd. BN7: Lew 2D **16**
Fullers Pas. BN7: Lew 4F **17**
Fullwood Av. BN9: New 4D **40**
Fulmar Cl. BN3: Hove 1B **28**
Fulmer Ct. BN11: Wor 2B **34**
Furlongs, The BN44: Stey 4C **4**
Furze Cl. BN13: High S 6B **6**
Furze Cft. BN3: Hove 4B **28**
Furzedene BN3: Hove 4B **28**
Furze Hill BN3: Hove 4B **28**
Furze Hill Ct. BN3: Hove 4B **28**
Furze Hill Ho. BN3: Hove 4C **28**
Furzeholme BN13: High S 6C **6**
Furze Rd. BN13: High S 6B **6**

G

Gableson Av. BN1: Brig 4H **11**
Gainsborough Av.
BN14: Broad 3E **21**
Gainsborough Ho. *BN3: Hove . . .3A 28*
(off Eaton Gdns.)
Gainsborough Lodge
BN14: Broad 6C **20**
Gaisford Cl. BN14: Wor 6C **20**
Gaisford Rd. BN14: Wor 6B **20**
Gala Bingo
Worthing **3C 34**
Galleries, The *BN3: Hove 3B 28*
(off Palmeira Av.)
Galliers Cl. BN1: Brig 2F **13**
Gallops, The BN7: Lew 4C **16**
Galsworthy Cl. BN12: Gor S 1D **32**
Galsworthy Rd. BN12: Gor S 1D **32**
Gannet Ho. BN3: Hove 1H **27**
Gannon Rd. BN11: Wor 1F **35**
Garcia Trad. Est. BN13: Wor 1H **33**
Garden Cl. BN15: Somp 4A **22**
BN41: Port 2C **26**
BN43: Shor S 1D **24**
Garden Ct. *BN3: Hove 3B 28*
(off Somerhill Av.)
BN43: Shor S 1D **24**
Gardener St. BN41: Port 2A **26**
Garden Ho., The BN1: Brig 3A **44**
Garden Pk. BN12: Fer 4A **32**
Gardens, The BN41: Port 2C **26**
BN42: S'wick 3H **25**
Garden St. BN7: Lew 5E **17**
Gardner Cen. Rd.
BN1: Falm 2D **14**
Gardner Rd. BN41: Port 3A **26**
Gardner St.
BN1: Brig 4C **44** (5E **29**)
Garland Point BN43: Shor B 4D **24**
Garnet Ho. *BN2: Brig 6G 29*
(off St George's Rd.)
Garrick Rd. BN14: Broad 6D **20**
Gatcombe Cl. BN13: Durr 5C **18**
Gatewycke Ter. *BN44: Stey 3C 4*
(off Tanyard La.)
Gaywood Wlk. BN13: Durr 5F **19**
Geneva Rd. BN9: New 5F **41**
George V Av. BN11: Wor 1H **33**
BN15: S Lan 5F **23**
George St. BN2: Brig . . .5D **44** (5E **29**)
BN3: Hove 4H **27**
BN41: Port 3A **26**
(Chapel Rd.)
BN41: Port 3C **26**
(Ellen St.)
George Williams M.
BN41: Port 2B **26**
Georgia Av. BN14: Broad 6D **20**
Gerald Rd. BN11: Wor 3H **33**
BN25: Sea 6E **43**
Gerard St. BN1: Brig 2E **29**
Ghyllside BN2: Brig 1A **30**
Gibbon Rd. BN9: New 5D **40**
Gibson Ct. BN7: Lew 3F **17**
Gildredge Rd. BN25: Sea 4E **43**
Girton Ho. BN3: Hove 4F **27**
Gladstone Ct. *BN2: Brig 2G 29*
(off Hartington Rd.)
Gladstone Pl. BN2: Brig 2G **29**
Gladstone Rd. BN41: Port 3B **26**
Gladstone Ter. BN2: Brig 3F **29**
Gladys Av. BN10: Peace 6H **39**
(not continuous)
Gladys Rd. BN3: Hove 2D **26**
Glastonbury Rd. BN3: Hove 4D **26**
Glawood Ho. BN14: Broad 4E **21**
Glebe Cl. BN7: Lew 5C **16**
BN15: Lan 3C **22**
BN42: S'wick 3G **25**
Glebe Dr. BN25: Sea 4D **42**
Glebelands Cl. BN43: Shor S . . .2D **24**
Glebe Rd. BN14: W Tar 5A **20**
Glebeside Av. BN14: Wor 5A **20**
Glebeside Cl. BN14: Wor 5A **20**
Glebe Vs. BN3: Hove 3D **26**
Glebe Way BN15: Lan 3C **22**
Glen, The BN13: Salv 3A **20**
Glenbarrie Way BN12: Fer 1A **32**
Glendale Rd. BN3: Hove 3B **28**
Glendor Rd. BN3: Hove 4E **27**
Gleneagles Cl. BN25: Sea 5H **41**
Glenfalls Av. BN1: Brig 1E **13**
Glen Gdns. BN12: Fer 2B **32**
Glen Ri. BN1: Brig 3H **11**
Glen Ri. Cl. BN1: Brig 3H **11**
Gleton Av. BN3: Hove 6D **10**
Gloucester Ct. *BN12: Gor S 3H 33*
(off George V Av.)
Gloucester M. BN1: Brig 3D **44**
Gloucester Pas. BN1: Brig 3D **44**
Gloucester Pl.
BN1: Brig 3D **44** (4E **29**)
Gloucester Rd.
BN1: Brig 3C **44** (4E **29**)
(not continuous)
Gloucester St.
BN1: Brig 3D **44** (4E **29**)
Gloucester Yd. *BN1: Brig 3D 44*
(off Gloucester Rd.)
Glover's Yd. BN1: Brig 1D **28**
Glynde Av. BN2: Salt 2B **38**
BN12: Gor S 4C **32**
(Amberley Dr.)
BN12: Gor S 2B **32**
(Thakeham Dr.)
Glyndebourne Av. BN2: Salt 2A **38**
Glyndebourne Ct.
BN43: Shor S 3B 24
(off Ham Rd.)
Glynde Cl. BN9: New 1F **41**
BN12: Fer 2B **32**
Glynde Ho. BN3: Hove 4B **28**
Glynde Rd. BN2: Brig 4H **29**
Glynleigh *BN2: Brig 4F 29*
(off Ashton Ri.)
Glynn Ri. BN10: Peace 3F **39**
Glynn Rd. BN10: Peace 3G **39**
Glynn Rd. W. BN10: Peace 3G **39**
Gochers Ct. *BN2: Brig 3G 29*
(off Islingword Rd.)
Godfrey Cl. BN7: Lew 2E **17**
Godstalls La. BN44: Stey 3B **4**
Godwin Rd. BN3: Hove 1D **26**
Golby Ct. BN10: Tel C 5E **39**
Golden La. BN1: Brig 5B **28**
Golden Sands Cvn. Pk.
BN15: S Lan 6E **23**
Gold La. BN10: Peace 2G **39**
Goldsmid M. *BN3: Hove 4B 28*
(off Farm M.)
Goldsmid Rd.
BN3: Hove 1A **44** (3C **28**)
Goldsmith Rd. BN14: Broad 6E **21**
Goldstone Cl. BN3: Hove 6G **11**
Goldstone Ct. BN3: Hove 5G **11**
Goldstone Cres. BN3: Hove 5G **11**
Goldstone Ho. *BN3: Hove 3H 27*
(off Clarendon Rd.)
Goldstone La. BN3: Hove 2H **27**
Goldstone Retail Pk.
BN3: Hove 2H **27**
Goldstone Rd. BN3: Hove 3H **27**
Goldstone St. BN3: Hove 3H **27**
Goldstone Vs. BN3: Hove 3H **27**
Goldstone Way BN3: Hove 6G **11**
Golf Dr. BN1: Brig 5F **13**
Goodwood Ct. BN3: Hove 3B **28**
Goodwood Rd. BN13: Salv 3A **20**
Goodwood Way BN2: Brig 5A **14**
Gordon Av. BN43: Shor S 3C **24**
Gordon Cl. BN41: Port 3C **26**
Gordon M. BN41: Port 3C **26**
Gordon Rd. BN1: Brig 6D **12**
BN11: Wor 1D **34**
BN15: Lan 4B **22**
BN41: Port 3A **26**
(Chapel Rd.)
BN41: Port 3C **26**
(Gordon Cl.)
BN43: Shor S 3B **24**
Gorham Av. BN2: Rott 2G **37**
Gorham Cl. BN2: Rott 2G **37**
Gorham Ct. BN10: Tel C 4C **38**
Gorham Way BN10: Tel C 4C **38**
Goring Bus. Pk. BN12: Gor S 1E **33**
GORING-BY-SEA 2E **33**
Goring-by-Sea Station (Rail) . . .1C **32**
Goring Chase BN12: Gor S 6C **18**
Goring Ct. BN1: Brig 3B **14**
BN44: Stey 4C 4
(off Bramber Rd.)
Goring Crossways
BN12: Gor S 6C **18**
GORING HALL BMI HOSPITAL
. . . .**2D 32**
Goring Rd. BN11: Wor 2E **33**
BN12: Gor S 2E **33**
BN44: Stey 4C **4**
Goring St. BN12: Gor S 6C **18**
Goring Way BN12: Fer, Gor S . . .2B **32**
BN12: Gor S 1D **32**
Gorringe Cl. BN43: Shor S 3F **25**
Gorse Av. BN14: Salv 4B **20**
BN16: King G 4A **32**
Gorse Cl. BN41: Port 4H **9**
Gorse Dr. BN25: Sea 1E **43**
Gorse La. BN13: High S 6C **6**
Gosling Cft. Bus. Cen.
BN13: Clap 2A **18**
Gosport Ct. *BN43: Shor B 4D 24*
(off Harbour Way)
Graffham Cl. BN2: Brig 4A **30**
Grafton Dr. BN15: Somp 4A **22**
Grafton Gdns. BN15: Somp 4A **22**
Grafton Pl. BN11: Wor 2D **34**
Grafton Rd. BN11: Wor 2D **34**
Grafton St. BN2: Brig 6F **29**
Graham Av. BN1: Brig 4C **12**
BN41: Port 4H **9**
Graham Cl. BN41: Port 4H **9**
Graham Ct. BN11: Wor 2H **33**
BN15: Somp 4A **22**
Graham Cres. BN41: Port 4H **9**
Graham Rd. BN11: Wor 2D **34**

A-Z Brighton & Worthing 53

Grand Av.—Headborough

Grand Av. BN3: Hove .5A 28
BN11: Wor .1A 34
BN15: Lan .4C 22
BN25: Sea .2B 42
Grand Av. Mans. *BN3: Hove .4A 28*
(off Grand Av.)
Grand Cres. BN2: Rott .3G 37
Grand Junc. Rd.
BN1: Brig .6C 44 (6E 29)
Grand Pde.
BN2: Brig .4D 44 (5E 29)
Grand Pde. M.
BN2: Brig .4D 44 (5E 29)
Grange, The .2G 37
Grange, The BN2: Salt .4B 38
Grange Cl. BN1: Brig .1C 28
BN12: Fer .3A 32
Grange Ct. *BN3: Hove .2F 27*
(off Payne Av.)
BN7: Lew .5E 17
BN12: Fer .2A 32
(off Ferring Grange Gdns.)
BN42: S'wick .3G 25
Grange Farm Cotts.
BN2: O'dean .6F 31
(off Greenways)
Grange Ind. Est., The
BN42: S'wick .3G 25
Grange Pk. BN12: Fer .3A 32
Grange Rd. BN3: Hove .3E 27
BN7: Lew .5E 17
BN42: S'wick .3G 25
Grange Wlk. BN1: Brig .3C 12
Grangeways BN1: Brig .3C 12
Grantham Rd. BN1: Brig .1E 29
Grantsmead BN15: N Lan .2C 22
Grant St. BN2: Brig .3F 29
Granville Ct. *BN3: Hove .3H 27*
(off Denmark Vs.)
BN25: Sea .5D 42
Granville Rd. BN3: Hove .3C 28
Graperies, The BN2: Brig .5G 29
Grasmere Av. BN15: Somp .4H 21
Grassmere Av. BN10: Tel C .4D 38
Grassmere Ct. BN10: Tel C .4E 39
Gratwicke Rd. BN11: Wor .2C 34
Gravelly Cres. BN15: Lan .4D 22
Gt. College St. BN2: Brig .6G 29
Greatham Ct. *BN1: Brig .2C 12*
(off Old London Rd.)
Greatham Rd. BN14: Fin V .1H 19
Great Wilkins BN1: Falm .3D 14
Green, The BN2: Rott .2F 37
BN3: Hove .6A 12
BN42: S'wick .3G 25
Greena Ct. BN11: Wor .2C 34
Greenacre BN10: Peace .2H 39
Greenacres BN1: Brig .1D 28
BN10: Tel C .5E 39
BN43: Shor S .2A 24
BN44: Stey .4C 4
Greenbank Av. BN2: Salt .3A 38
Green Cl. BN42: S'wick .3G 25
Green Ct. *BN42: S'wick .3G 25*
(off The Green)
Greene Ct. BN7: Lew .5D 16
Greenfield Cl. BN1: Brig .3E 13
BN42: S'wick .2G 25
Greenfield Cres. BN1: Brig .3D 12
Green Ga. BN10: Peace .3G 39
Greenhill Way BN10: Peace .2G 39
Greenland Cl. BN13: Durr .3G 19
Greenland Rd. BN13: Durr .4F 19
Greenland Wlk. BN13: Durr .3G 19
Green La. BN2: W'dean .4G 31
BN7: Lew .5E 17
BN25: Sea .5D 42
Greenleas BN3: Hove .6D 10
Greenleaves BN44: Bramb .5D 4
Greenoaks BN15: N Lan .2B 22
Green Pk. BN12: Fer .1B 32
Green Ridge BN1: Brig .3H 11
Greentrees BN11: Wor .2B 34
BN15: Somp .5A 22
Greentrees Cl. BN15: Somp .4A 22
Greentrees Cres.
BN15: Somp .4A 22
Green Wlk. BN25: Sea .5G 43
Green Wall BN7: Lew .4F 17
Greenway, The BN12: Gor S .6D 18
Greenway Ct. BN2: Rott .3G 37
Greenways BN2: O'dean .6F 31
BN41: Port .1B 26
BN42: S'wick .1H 25
Greenways Cnr. BN2: O'dean .6E 31
Greenways Cres. BN12: Fer .3B 32
BN43: Shor S .1C 24
Greenwell Cl. BN25: Sea .3G 43
Greenwich Way BN10: Peace .5F 39
Greet Rd. BN15: Lan .3B 22
Grenville Av. BN12: Gor S .1F 33
Grenville Cl. BN12: Gor S .1E 33
Grenville Ho. BN10: Peace .3H 39
Grenville St.
BN1: Brig .5B 44 (5D 28)
Greyfriars BN3: Hove .2B 28
Greyfriars Cl. BN13: Salv .4A 20
Greyfriars Ct. BN7: Lew .4F 17
Grey Point Ho. BN14: Fin .2C 6
Greystoke M. BN12: Fer .2A 32
Greystoke Rd. BN12: Fer .2A 32
Greystone Av. BN13: Wor .5H 19
Griffiths Av. BN15: N Lan .2B 22
Grinstead Av. BN15: Lan .4C 22
Grinstead La. BN15: Lan .5C 22
Grinstead Mt. BN2: Brig .5B 30
Grosvenor Ct. BN1: Brig .5C 12
BN25: Sea .4C 42
Grosvenor Mans. BN3: Hove .4H 27
Grosvenor M. BN25: Sea .3C 42
Grosvenor Rd. BN11: Wor .2D 34
BN25: Sea .4C 42
Grosvenor St. BN2: Brig .5F 29
Grove, The BN9: New .1G 41
BN12: Fer .2A 32
Grove Bank *BN2: Brig .4F 29*
(off Albion St.)
Grove Ct. BN3: Hove .4A 28
Grove Hill BN2: Brig .4F 29
Grovelands, The BN15: S Lan .6C 22
Grove Lodge BN14: Broad .4C 20
Grove Lodge Rdbt.
BN14: Broad .3C 20
Grover Av. BN15: Lan .3B 22
Grove Rd. BN14: Broad .4C 20
BN25: Sea .4E 43
Grove St. BN2: Brig .4F 29
Grove Villa *BN1: Brig .3D 28*
(off New England Rd.)
Grub Ride BN13: Clap .6A 6
Guardian Ct. BN13: Salv .4A 20
Guardswell Pl. BN25: Sea .4E 43
Guernsey Rd. BN12: Fer .4B 32
Guildbourne Cen., The
BN11: Wor .2D 34
Guildford Cl. BN14: Wor .6A 20
Guildford Rd.
BN1: Brig .2B 44 (4D 28)
BN14: Wor .1A 34
Guildford St.
BN1: Brig .2B 44 (4D 28)
Guinness Ct. BN9: New .1G 41
Guinness Trust Bungs.
BN9: S Heig .1G 41
(off Iveagh Cres.)
BN9: S Heig .1G 41
(Port Vw.)
Gundreda Rd. BN7: Lew .3C 16
Gwydyr Mans. BN3: Hove .4B 28

H

Haddington Cl. BN3: Hove .4H 27
Haddington St. BN3: Hove .3H 27
Hadley Av. BN14: Broad .3D 20
Hadlow Cl. BN2: Brig .4H 29
Hadlow Way BN15: Lan .4D 22
Hadrian Av. BN42: S'wick .2A 26
Haig Av. BN1: Brig .2H 13
Haigh Cl. BN15: S Lan .4F 23
Hailsham Av. BN2: Salt .1B 38
Hailsham Rd. BN11: Wor .3H 33
Hairpin Cft. BN10: Peace .3G 39
Halewick Cl. BN15: Somp .2A 22
Halewick La. BN15: Somp .2A 22
Half Moon Ct. *BN13: Salv .3H 19*
(off Half Moon La.)
Half Moon La. BN13: Salv .2H 19
Half Moon Pde. *BN13: Salv .3H 19*
(off Half Moon La.)
Halifax Dr. BN13: Durr .4E 19
Halland Rd. BN2: Brig .4B 14
Hall Av. BN14: Salv .3A 20
Hall Cl. BN14: Salv .3A 20
Hallett Rd. BN2: Brig .3H 29
Hallyburton Rd. BN3: Hove .2D 26
Halsbury Cl. BN11: Wor .1E 35
Halsbury Rd. BN11: Wor .1F 35
Hamble Ct. BN15: Somp .4H 21
Hamble Gdns. BN13: Durr .3E 19
Hamble Rd. BN15: Somp .4H 21
Hamble Way BN13: Durr .3E 19
Ham Bri. Trad. Est.
BN14: Broad .6G 21
Ham Bus. Cen. BN43: Shor S .3C 24
Ham Cl. BN11: Wor .6G 21
Hamfield Av. BN43: Shor S .2B 24
Hamilton Cl. BN14: Broad .5E 21
BN41: Port .5A 10
Hamilton Ct. BN2: Brig .1A 36
BN12: Gor S .6F 19
(off Drake Av.)
Hamilton Ho. BN25: Sea .3D 42
Hamilton Mans. BN3: Hove .5H 27
Hamilton M. BN15: Somp .4A 22
Hamilton Rd. BN1: Brig .2D 28
BN15: Lan .3B 22
Ham La. BN7: Lew .5F 17
Hammond Dr. BN13: Durr .2G 19
Hammy Cl. BN43: Shor S .2D 24
Hammy La. BN43: Shor S .2D 24
Hammy Way BN43: Shor S .2D 24
Hampden Ct. BN11: Wor .6F 21
Hampden Gdns. BN9: S Heig .1F 41
Hampden Rd. BN2: Brig .3G 29
Hampshire Ct. BN2: Brig .6F 29
Hampstead Rd. BN1: Brig .1B 28
Hampton Pl. BN1: Brig .5C 28
Hampton St.
BN1: Brig .4A 44 (5C 28)
Hampton Ter. *BN1: Brig .3A 44*
(off Upper Nth. St.)
Ham Rd. BN11: Wor .6G 21
BN43: Shor S .3B 24
Hamsey Cl. BN2: Brig .5B 30
Hamsey Cres. BN7: Lew .3B 16
Hamsey La. BN25: Sea .5H 43
Hamsey Rd. BN2: Salt .3B 38
Ham Way BN11: Wor .6G 21
Hancock Way BN43: Shor B .4D 24
HANGLETON
BN3 .6E 11
BN12 .6A 18
Hangleton Cl. BN3: Hove .6D 10
Hangleton Gdns. BN3: Hove .1D 26
Hangleton Grange BN12: Fer .1A 32
Hangleton La. BN3: Hove .6C 10
BN12: Fer .1A 32
BN41: Port .6B 10
(not continuous)
Hangleton Link Rd.
BN41: Port .5C 10
Hangleton Mnr. Cl.
BN3: Hove .6C 10
Hangleton Rd. BN3: Hove .2D 26
Hangleton Valley Dr.
BN3: Hove .6C 10
Hangleton Way BN3: Hove .1D 26
Hanover Cl. BN25: Sea .1A 42
Hanover Ct. BN2: Brig .3F 29
BN14: Broad .4C 20
(off Rectory Gdns.)
Hanover Cres. BN2: Brig .3F 29
Hanover Lofts *BN2: Brig .4F 29*
(off Finsbury Rd.)
Hanover M. BN2: Brig .3F 29
Hanover Pl. *BN2: Brig .3F 29*
(off Lewes Rd.)
Hanover St. BN2: Brig .3F 29
Hanover Ter. BN2: Brig .3F 29
Hanson Rd. BN9: New .5D 40
Happy Days Cvn. Pk.
BN15: S Lan .5E 23
Harbour Ct. *BN42: S'wick .3H 25*
(off Whiterock Pl.)
HARBOUR HEIGHTS .6D 40
Harbour Ho. BN43: Shor B .4D 24
Harbour Vw. Cl. BN9: New .5D 40
BN25: Sea .1A 42
Harbour Vw. Rd. BN9: New .6D 40
Harbour Way BN43: Shor B .4C 24
Hardwicke Ho. *BN25: Sea .5D 42*
(off Esplanade)
Hardwick Gdns. *.5D 42*
(off Esplanade)
Hardwick Rd. BN3: Hove .5E 11
Hardwick Way BN3: Hove .5E 11
(not continuous)
Hardy Cl. BN43: Shor B .4B 24
Harebell Dr. BN41: Port .5A 10
Harefield Av. BN13: Wor .6H 19
Harewood Ct. BN3: Hove .4A 28
Harfield Cl. BN9: New .1H 41
Harison Rd. BN25: Sea .3F 43
Harlech Cl. BN13: Durr .5D 18
Harley Ct. BN11: Wor .2B 34
Harmsworth Cres. BN3: Hove .5E 11
Harpers Rd. BN9: New .4E 41
Harriet Pl. BN43: Shor B .4D 24
Harrington Ct. BN1: Brig .6C 12
Harrington Mans. BN1: Brig .6C 12
Harrington Pl. BN1: Brig .6F 13
Harrington Rd. BN1: Brig .6C 12
Harrington Vs. BN1: Brig .6D 12
Harrison Ct. BN14: Broad .5E 21
Harrison Rd. BN14: Broad .5E 21
Harrow Cl. BN25: Sea .3F 43
Harrow Rd. BN11: Wor .1B 34
Hartfield Av. BN1: Brig .4E 13
Hartfield Ct. BN3: Hove .4A 28
Hartfield Rd. BN2: Salt .3B 38
BN25: Sea .4F 43
Harting Cl. BN12: Gor S .6D 18
Hartington Pl. BN2: Brig .2G 29
Hartington Rd. BN2: Brig .2G 29
Hartington Ter. BN2: Brig .2G 29
Hartington Vs. BN3: Hove .2H 27
Hartland Ho. *BN11: Wor .2A 34*
(off Southview Dr.)
Hartley Ct. *BN1: Brig .1B 44*
(off Howard Pl.)
Harvard Cl. BN7: Lew .2E 17
Harvest Cl. BN10: Tel C .2F 39
Harvey Rd. BN12: Gor S .3G 33
Harvey's Way BN7: Lew .4G 17
Harwood Av. BN12: Gor S .6F 19
Hastings Av. BN25: Sea .2H 43
Hastings Ct. BN11: Wor .3A 34
Hastings Rd. BN2: Brig .2G 29
BN11: Wor .3A 34
Hatfield Wlk. BN13: Durr .5F 19
Havelock Rd. BN1: Brig .6D 12
Haven, The BN15: S Lan .6D 22
Haven Brow BN25: Sea .3F 43
Havenside BN43: Shor B .4A 24
Haven Way BN9: New .5D 40
Havercroft Bldgs. BN11: Wor .2D 34
Hawkenbury Way BN7: Lew .4C 16
Hawkhurst Pl. BN1: Brig .2H 13
Hawkhurst Rd. BN1: Brig .1H 13
Hawkins Cl. BN43: Shor S .1F 25
Hawkins Cres. BN43: Shor S .6F 9
Hawkins Rd. BN43: Shor S .1F 25
Hawth Cl. BN25: Sea .3B 42
Hawth Cres. BN25: Sea .3B 42
Hawth Gro. BN25: Sea .2B 42
Hawth Hill BN25: Sea .2A 42
Hawthorn Bank BN2: Brig .4B 14
Hawthorn Cl. BN2: Salt .2A 38
Hawthorn Cres. BN14: Broad .4D 20
Hawthorn Est. BN9: New .3G 41
Hawthorn Gdns. BN14: Broad .4D 20
Hawthorn Ri. BN9: New .4D 40
Hawthorn Rd. BN14: Broad .4D 20
Hawthorn Way BN41: Port .5A 10
Hawth Pk. Rd. BN25: Sea .3B 42
Hawth Pl. BN25: Sea .3B 42
Hawth Ri. BN25: Sea .2B 42
Hawth Valley Ct. BN25: Sea .3B 42
Hawth Way BN25: Sea .3C 42
Haybourne Cl. BN2: Brig .3A 30
Haybourne Rd. BN2: Brig .3A 30
Hayes Cl. BN41: Port .2C 26
Hayley Rd. BN15: Lan .3D 22
Hayling Gdns. BN13: High S .1G 19
Hayling Ri. BN13: High S .1G 19
Haynes Rd. BN14: Wor .6A 20
Haynes Way BN14: Wor .6B 20
Hayton Ct. *BN13: Durr .5D 18*
(off Chestnut Wlk.)
Hayward Rd. BN7: Lew .2C 16
Haywards Rd. BN1: Brig .2E 13
Hazel Bank *BN2: Brig .3F 29*
(off Bromley Rd.)
Hazel Cl. BN9: New .4D 40
BN41: Port .5C 10
Hazeldene BN25: Sea .4G 43
Hazeldene Meads BN1: Brig .5B 12
Hazel Holt BN41: Port .5H 9
Hazelhurst Cres. BN14: Fin V .5D 6
Hazelwood *BN1: Brig .5B 12*
(off Curwen Pl.)
Hazelwood Cl. BN14: Broad .5F 21
Hazelwood Lodge
BN15: S Lan .5D 22
Hazelwood Trad. Est.
BN14: Broad .5F 21
Headborough *BN15: S Lan .6C 22*
(off Alma St.)

Headborough Ct. BN15: S Lan 6C 22
Headland Av. BN25: Sea 4F 43
Headland Cl. BN10: Peace 4A 40
Headland Cnr. *BN25: Sea* *5F 43*
(off Headland Av.)
Headland Way BN10: Peace ...5A 40
Heathdown Ct. BN10: Peace ...2G 39
Heather Ct. BN1: Brig 4C 28
Heather Ho. BN15: Lan 3D 22
Heather La. BN13: High S 6C 6
Heatherstone Rd. BN11: Wor ..1G 35
Heathfield Av. BN2: Salt 2B 38
Heathfield Cl. BN13: Wor 5H 19
Heathfield Cres. BN41: Port 4H 9
Heathfield Dr. BN41: Port 5H 9
Heathfield Rd. BN25: Sea 5E 43
Heath Hill Av. BN2: Brig 6B 14
HEATHY BROW 3F 39
Heathy Brow
BN10: Peace, Tel C 3F 39
Hebe Rd. BN43: Shor S 3A 24
HEENE 1B 34
Heene Pl. BN11: Wor 3B 34
Heene Rd. BN11: Wor 1B 34
Heene Ter. BN11: Wor 3B 34
Heene Way BN11: Wor 2B 34
Heighton Cres. BN9: New ...1F 41
Heighton Rd.
BN9: New, S Heig 1F 41
Heights, The BN1: Brig 3H 11
BN14: Fin V 1A 20
Helena Cl. BN41: Port 6C 10
Helena Rd. BN2: W'dean 1E 31
Helen Ct. BN11: Wor 2H 33
Hellingly Cl. BN2: Brig 5B 30
Hempstead Rd. BN2: Salt 1B 38
Henderson Wlk. BN44: Stey ...2C 4
Hendon St. BN2: Brig 5H 29
Henfield Cl. BN2: Brig 5B 30
BN12: Gor S 6E 19
Henfield Rd. BN5: S Dole ...5G 5
BN44: Up B 5G 5
Henfield Way BN3: Hove 5F 11
Henge Way BN41: Port 6B 10
Henley Ct. BN2: Brig 4B 36
Henley Rd. BN2: Brig 4B 36
Henty Cl. BN14: Wor 6C 20
Henty Rd. BN12: Fer 4B 32
BN14: Wor 6C 20
Herbert Rd. BN1: Brig 6D 12
BN15: Somp 1H 21
Hereford Ct. BN2: Brig 5G 29
BN3: Hove 3A 28
Hereford Ho. *BN12: Gor S* *1C 32*
(off Goring St.)
Hereford St. BN2: Brig 5F 29
Hereward Way BN7: Lew 2F 17
Hermione Cl. BN12: Fer 1A 32
Hermit Ter. BN14: Fin 2C 6
Herm Rd. BN12: Fer 4B 32
Heron Ct. *BN2: Brig* *3B 30*
(off Swanborough Pl.)
BN11: Wor 1C 34
Herons, The BN15: S Lan ...6D 22
BN43: Shor S 2C 24
Heronsdale Rd. BN2: W'dean ..2H 31
Hertford Rd. BN1: Brig 6F 13
BN11: Wor 1D 34
Heston Av. BN1: Brig 1D 12
Heyshott Cl. BN15: N Lan 2C 22
Heyshott Lodge *BN2: Brig* *4A 30*
(off Crossbush Rd.)
Heyworth Cl. BN2: W'dean ...2H 31
Highbank BN1: Brig 3A 12
Highbarn BN14: Fin 1C 6
High Beach Ho. BN25: Sea ...4B 42
High Beeches BN11: Wor 2A 34
Highbrook Cl. BN2: Brig 6H 13
Highclere Way BN13: Durr ...5D 18
Highcliff Ct. BN2: Rott 3G 37
High Cl. BN41: Port 1A 26
Highcroft Lodge BN1: Brig ...2C 28
Highcroft M. BN1: Brig 1B 28
Highcroft Vs. BN1: Brig 2C 28
Highden BN2: Brig 4G 29
Highdown Cl. BN15: Wor 1H 25
Highdown Av. BN13: W Tar ...5A 20
Highdown Cl. BN12: Fer 1A 32
BN42: S'wick 1H 25
Highdown Ct. BN1: Brig 5C 12
BN13: Durr 5F 19
Highdown Gdns. 5B 18
Highdown Hill 5A 18
Highdown Rd. BN3: Hove ...3C 28
BN7: Lew 3B 16

Highdown Way BN12: Fer 1A 32
Highfield Cl. BN14: Broad 4E 21
Highfield Cres. BN1: Brig 3E 13
Highfield Rd. BN13: W Tar ...4A 20
Highfields BN1: Brig 3A 14
Highgrove Gdns. BN11: Wor ..2B 34
Highland Cft. BN44: Stey 3C 4
Highlands Cl. BN13: High S ...1G 19
Highlands Rd. BN25: Sea 4E 43
BN41: Port 1B 26
Highleigh BN2: Brig 4F 29
High Pk. Av. BN3: Hove 5E 11
High Pines BN11: Wor 1B 34
HIGH SALVINGTON 6C 6
High Salvington Windmill 6C 6
Highsted Pk. BN10: Peace ...2H 39
High St. BN2: Brig 5F 29
BN2: Rott 3F 37
BN7: Lew 5E 17
BN9: New 4E 41
BN11: Wor 2E 35
(Charlecote La.)
BN11: Wor 1E 35
(Markwick M.)
BN14: Fin 3C 6
BN14: W Tar 5A 20
BN25: Sea 5D 42
BN41: Port 1A 26
BN43: Shor S 3A 24
BN44: Stey 3B 4
BN44: Up B 4F 5
High Vw. BN13: High S 1H 19
Highview Av. Nth. BN1: Brig ..2C 12
Highview Av. Sth. BN1: Brig ..2C 12
High Vw. Rd. BN10: Tel C ...4C 38
Highview Rd. BN1: Brig 2C 12
Highview Way BN1: Brig 2C 12
Highway, The BN2: Brig 6H 13
(Highway Cl., not continuous)
BN2: Brig 6H 13
(Southall Av., not continuous)
BN9: New, Peace 5D 40
BN10: New, Peace 5B 40
Highway Cl. BN2: Brig 6H 13
Highways BN41: Port 6B 10
Hilary Lodge BN2: Brig 5G 29
Hildon Cl. BN13: Durr 5F 19
Hildon Pk. BN13: Durr 5F 19
Hilgrove Rd. BN2: Salt 1B 38
Hillbank Cl. BN41: Port 5H 9
Hillbank M. BN15: Somp 1B 22
Hillbarn Pde. *BN15: Somp* *2A 22*
(off Up. Brighton Rd.)
Hill Brow BN3: Hove 4H 11
Hillbrow Rd. BN1: Brig 4A 12
Hillcrest BN1: Brig 3A 12
Hill Crest Cl. BN9: New 5E 41
Hillcrest Ct. BN1: Brig 3A 12
Hill Crest Rd. BN9: New 5E 41
Hillcroft BN41: Port 6H 9
Hill Dr. BN3: Hove 4H 11
Hill Farm Cotts. BN42: S'wick ..6F 9
Hill Farm Way BN42: S'wick ...6F 9
Hillman Cl. BN7: Lew 4G 17
Hill Ri. BN9: New 1H 41
Hillrise Av. BN15: Somp 2A 22
Hill Rd. BN2: Salt 3H 37
BN7: Lew 3C 16
BN9: New 2H 41
BN10: Peace 6B 40
Hillside BN2: Brig 5A 14
BN9: New 4F 41
BN13: Pat 1A 18
BN41: Port 1C 26
BN42: S'wick 1G 25
Hillside Av. BN14: Char D 3B 20
BN25: Sea 2H 43
Hillside Cotts. BN13: Pat 1A 18
Hillside Rd. BN15: Somp 2A 22
Hillside Ter. BN44: Stey 4C 4
Hillside Way BN1: Brig 4A 12
BN2: Brig 6A 14
Hills Rd. BN44: Stey 3B 4
Hilltop BN1: Brig 3H 11
Hill Top Way BN9: New 5D 40
Hillview Ho. BN9: New 5F 41
Hillview Rd. BN14: Fin V 1H 19
Hillview Rd. BN2: W'dean ...2D 30
Hillyfield BN7: Lew 5D 16
Hindover Cres. BN25: Sea ...3F 43
Hindover Rd. BN25: Sea 3F 43

Hinton Cl. BN1: Brig 6G 13
HMP Lewes BN7: Lew 4C 16
Hoathdown Av. BN9: New ...4C 40
Hobart Cl. BN13: Durr 3E 19
Hobs Acre BN44: Up B 5G 5
Hoddern Av. BN10: Peace ...5F 39
(not continuous)
Hodshrove La. BN2: Brig 5A 14
Hodshrove Pl. BN2: Brig 5A 14
Hodshrove Rd. BN2: Brig 5A 14
Hoe Ct. BN15: N Lan 1D 22
Hogarth Rd. BN3: Hove 3F 27
Hogs Edge BN2: Brig 6C 14
Holbrook *BN2: Brig* *5B 30*
(off Findon Rd.)
Holland M. BN3: Hove 5B 28
Holland Rd. BN3: Hove 5B 28
BN44: Stey 3D 4
Holland St. BN2: Brig 4F 29
Hollingbourne Ct. *BN2: Brig* ...*4A 36*
(off Bristol Pl.)
HOLLINGBURY 4E 13
Hollingbury Copse BN1: Brig ..4E 13
Hollingbury Cres. BN1: Brig ..6F 13
Hollingbury Gdns. BN14: Fin V ..5E 7
Hollingbury Ind. Est.
BN1: Brig 1G 13
Hollingbury Pk. Av. BN1: Brig ..6E 13
Hollingbury Pl. BN1: Brig 6E 13
Hollingbury Ri. BN1: Brig 5F 13
Hollingbury Ri. W. BN1: Brig ..5F 13
Hollingbury Rd. BN1: Brig 6E 13
Hollingbury Ter. BN1: Brig ...6E 13
HOLLINGDEAN 6F 13
Hollingdean La. BN1: Brig 2F 29
Hollingdean Rd. BN2: Brig ...2F 29
Hollingdean St. BN2: Brig 1F 29
Hollingdean Ter. BN1: Brig ...1F 29
Hollow, The BN9: S Heig 1F 41
Hollyacres BN13: Durr 2F 19
Holly Bank *BN2: Brig* *2F 29*
(off Bromley Rd.)
Holly Cl. BN1: Brig 5C 12
BN13: Durr 5E 19
Holmbush Cen., The
BN43: Shor S 6E 9
Holmbush Cl. BN43: Shor S ..2E 25
Holmbush Way BN42: S'wick ..1F 25
Holmcroft Gdns. BN14: Fin ...2C 6
Holmdale Rd. BN9: New 2H 41
Holmes Av. BN3: Hove 1F 27
Holmes Cl. BN25: Sea 5H 41
Holmstead BN2: Brig 3F 29
Holt, The BN25: Sea 2D 42
Holters Way BN15: Lan 2E 43
Holt Lodge *BN2: Brig* *2F 29*
(off Canterbury Dr.)
Holton Hill BN2: W'dean 3G 31
Holtview Rd. BN2: W'dean ...2D 30
Homebush Av. BN2: Salt 3B 38
BN7: Tel C 1D 38
Homecoast Ho. BN10: Peace ..5F 39
Homedrive Ho. BN3: Hove ...2A 28
Home Farm Bus. Cen.
BN1: Brig 5H 13
Home Farm Rd. BN1: Brig ...5H 13
Homefield Cl. BN25: Sea 3E 43
Homefield Rd. BN11: Wor 1E 35
BN25: Sea 3E 43
Homehaven Ct. BN43: Shor S ..3A 24
Homeleigh BN1: Brig 3B 12
Homepier Ho. BN11: Wor ...2B 34
Homeridge Ho. BN2: Salt 3A 38
Home Rd. BN1: Brig 6C 12
Homesearle Ho. BN12: Gor S ..2E 33
Homestead Cotts. BN12: Fer ..2B 32
Homestead M. BN12: Fer 2B 32
Hometeye Ho. BN14: Broad ..6D 20
Hometye Ho. BN25: Sea 3C 42
Homewood BN14: Fin 1C 6
Honey Cft. BN9: New 5D 10
Honeysuckle Cl. BN15: N Lan ..1B 22
Honeysuckle La. BN13: High S ..4A 6
Hoopers Cl. BN7: Lew 2E 17
Hope Cotts. BN42: S'wick ...2G 25
Hopedene Ct. BN11: Wor ...2C 34
Hopewell Cl. BN43: Shor B ...4D 24
Horatio Ho. BN1: Brig 2C 44
Horizon Cl. BN41: Port 2B 26
Horizon Ri. BN3: Hove 4F 27
(off Kingsway)
Horley Pl. BN2: Brig 4A 30
Hornby Pl. *BN2: Brig* *1C 30*
(off Hornby Rd.)

Hornby Rd. BN2: Brig 1B 30
Horeshoe Cl. BN14: Fin 2C 6
Horsfield Rd. BN7: Lew 2D 16
Horsham Av. BN10: Peace ...6F 39
(not continuous)
Horsham Av. Nth.
BN10: Peace 4G 39
Horsham Cl. BN2: Brig 4B 30
Horsham Rd. BN14: Fin 1C 6
BN44: Stey 1B 4
(not continuous)
Horsted Ct. BN1: Brig 1C 44
Horton Cl. BN11: Wor 1F 35
Horton Rd. BN1: Brig 1F 29
Houndean Cl. BN7: Lew 5C 16
Houndean Rd. BN7: Lew 5B 16
Hova Vs. BN3: Hove 4H 27
HOVE 4H 27
Hove Bus. Cen. BN3: Hove ...2H 27
Hovedene BN3: Hove 3A 28
Hove Ent. Cen. BN41: Port ...4C 26
Hove Lagoon Watersports ...4D 26
Hove Mnr. BN3: Hove 4G 27
Hove Mus. & Art Gallery 4G 27
Hove Pk. Gdns. BN3: Hove ...1H 27
Hove Pk. Rd. BN3: Hove 1H 27
Hove Pk. Vs. BN3: Hove 2H 27
Hove Pk. Way BN3: Hove ...1A 28
Hove Pl. BN3: Hove 5H 27
HOVE POLYCLINIC 1F 27
Hove Seaside Vs.
BN41: Port 4D 26
Hove Sea Wall BN3: Hove ...5A 28
Hove Station (Rail) 2H 27
Hove St. BN3: Hove 4G 27
Hove St. Sth. BN3: Hove 5G 27
Howard Ct. BN3: Hove 6F 11
BN10: Peace 5F 39
Howard Ho. BN10: Peace ...3H 39
Howard Pl. BN1: Brig ...1A 44 (3D 28)
Howard Rd. BN2: Brig 5F 29
BN15: Somp 1H 21
Howard St. BN11: Wor 1C 34
Howard Ter. BN1: Brig ...1A 44 (3D 28)
Howey Cl. BN9: New 2H 41
Hoyle Rd. BN10: Peace 5G 39
Hudson Cl. BN13: Durr 4F 19
Hughes Rd. BN2: Brig 2F 29
Humber Av. BN13: Durr 3E 19
Humber Cl. BN13: Durr 3E 19
Humphrey's Gap
BN43: Shor S 3C 24
Humphry's Almshouses
BN11: Wor *2D 34*
(off Humphrys Rd.)
Humphrys Rd. BN11: Wor ...2D 34
Hunston Cl. BN2: W'dean 3H 31
Huntington Ct. *BN7: Lew* *4G 17*
(off Malling St.)
Hurdis Rd. BN25: Sea 1A 42
Hurley Rd. BN13: Durr 4G 19
Hurst Av. BN11: Wor 2H 33
Hurst Ct. *BN1: Brig* *1B 28*
(off Reigate Rd.)
Hurst Cres. BN41: Port 2B 26
Hurstfield BN15: Lan 5B 22
Hurst Hill BN1: Brig 3G 13
Hurston Cl. BN14: Fin V 2A 20
Hurstwood BN2: Brig 5B 30
Hutton Rd. BN1: Brig 5F 13
Hyde, The BN2: Brig 1B 30
Hyde Bus. Pk., The BN2: Brig ...1C 30
Hyde La. BN44: Up B 4G 5
Hyde Sq. BN44: Up B 4G 5
Hyde St. BN44: Up B 4G 5
Hylden Cl. BN2: W'dean 2D 30
Hythe Cl. BN11: Wor 3A 34
BN25: Sea 2H 43
Hythe Cres. BN25: Sea 3H 43
Hythe Rd. BN1: Brig 6E 13
BN11: Wor 3A 34
Hythe Vw. BN25: Sea 3H 43

I

Iden Cl. BN2: Brig 5A 30
Ifield Cl. BN2: Salt 2C 38
Iford Cl. BN9: New 1F 41
Ilex Cl. BN42: S'wick 1A 26
Ilex Ct. *BN12: Gor S* *2D 32*
(off Goring St.)
Ilex Way BN12: Gor S 2D 32
Imperial Arc.
BN1: Brig 4A 44 (5D 28)

Larkfield Way BN1: Brig ...4E 13
Lark Hill BN3: Hove ...5E 11
Latimer Ct. *BN11: Wor* ...*3H 33*
   (off Latimer Rd.)
Latimer Rd. BN11: Wor ...3H 33
Laughton Rd. BN2: W'dean ...2H 31
Laurel Cl. BN13: Durr ...5E 19
Laurels, The *BN2: Brig* ...*2F 29*
   (off Bromley Rd.)
Laurens Wlk. Shop. Arc.
   BN2: Rott ...*3F 37*
   (off Nevill Rd.)
Laurier Ct. BN14: Broad ...6D 20
Lauriston Rd. BN1: Brig ...6C 12
Lavant Cl. BN12: Gor S ...6C 18
Lavender Hill BN43: Shor S ...1D 24
Lavender Ho. *BN2: Brig* ...*6F 29*
   (off Lavender St.)
Lavender St. BN2: Brig ...6F 29
Lavington Rd. BN14: Wor ...4B 20
Lavinia Ct. BN12: Gor S ...1E 33
Lawes Av. BN3: New ...4E 41
Lawns, The BN15: Somp ...3H 21
Lawrence Rd. BN3: Hove ...3F 27
Laylands Ct. *BN41: Port* ...*3A 26*
   (off Chapel Rd.)
Laylands Rd. BN41: Port ...3A 26
Leach Ct. BN2: Brig ...5G 29
Leahurst Ct. BN1: Brig ...5B 12
Leahurst Ct. Rd. BN1: Brig ...5B 12
Lea Rd. BN10: Peace ...4F 39
Leas, The BN10: Peace ...6B 40
Leconfield Rd. BN15: Lan ...5A 22
Lee Bank *BN2: Brig* ...*4F 29*
   (off Grove Hill)
Lee Ct. *BN9: New* ...
   (off Elphick Rd.)
Leeds Cl. BN13: Durr ...5D 18
Lee Rd. BN7: Lew ...3D 16
Leeward Cl. BN13: W Tar ...5H 19
Leeward Rd. BN13: W Tar ...5H 19
Lee Way BN9: New ...3E 41
Leicester Ct. BN7: Lew ...4D 16
Leicester St. BN2: Brig ...5F 29
Leicester Vs. BN3: Hove ...3D 26
Leigh Rd. BN14: Broad ...4D 20
Leighside Ho. *BN7: Lew* ...*4F 17*
   (off Court Rd.)
Leighton Av. BN14: Broad ...4E 21
Leighton Rd. BN3: Hove ...2G 27
Lenham Av. BN2: Salt ...3H 37
Lenham Rd. E.
   BN2: Rott, Salt ...3H 37
Lenham Rd. W. BN2: Rott ...3G 37
Lenhurst Way BN13: Wor ...6H 19
Lennox M. *BN11: Wor* ...*1D 34*
   (off Chapel Rd.)
Lennox Rd. BN3: Hove ...2F 27
   BN11: Wor ...1D 34
   BN43: Shor S ...2D 24
Lennox St. BN2: Brig ...5F 29
Leopold Rd.
   BN1: Brig ...3A **44** (4D **28**)
Lesser Foxholes
   BN43: Shor S ...1H 23
Letchworth Cl. BN12: Fer ...3A 32
Level, The ...3F 29
LEWES ...4F 17
Lewes Athletics Track ...5G 17
Lewes Bus. Cen. & Waterside Cen.
   BN7: Lew ...3E 17
Lewes Castle ...4E 17
Lewes Cl. BN2: Salt ...3C 38
Lewes Cres. BN2: Brig ...4A 36
   (not continuous)
Lewes FC ...5F 17
Lewes Leisure Cen. ...5G 17
Lewes Little Theatre ...4F 17
Lewes M. *BN2: Brig* ...*4A 36*
   (off Arundel Pl.)
Lewes Priory ...5E 17
Lewes Railway Land Local
   Nature Reserve ...5G 17
Lewes Rd. BN1: Brig ...1G 29
   BN2: Brig ...4F 29
   BN9: New ...2D 40
Lewes Southern By-Pass
   BN7: Lew ...6B 16
   BN8: Lew ...6B 16
Lewes Station (Rail) ...5F 17
Lewes St. BN2: Brig ...4F 29
Lewin Cl. BN15: Lan ...3D 22
Lewis Cl. BN9: New ...1H 41
Lewis Ct. BN13: Durr ...5D 18
Lewis Rd. BN15: N Lan ...2B 22

Lewis's Bldgs. BN1: Brig ...4B 44
Lewry Cl. BN1: Brig ...4D 40
Lexden Ct. BN25: Sea ...3F 43
Lexden Dr. BN25: Sea ...2E 43
Lexden Rd. BN25: Sea ...1E 43
Leybourne Cl. BN2: Brig ...1C 30
Leybourne Pde. *BN2: Brig* ...*1C 30*
   (off Leybourne Rd.)
Leybourne Rd. BN2: Brig ...6C 14
Library Pl. BN11: Wor ...2E 35
Library Rd. BN1: Falm ...1D 14
Lichfield Ct. BN2: Brig ...5B 30
   BN11: Wor ...3A 34
Lido, The ...3D 34
Lilac Cl. BN13: Durr ...5D 18
Lilac Ct. BN1: Brig ...4B 12
Limbrick Cl. BN12: Gor S ...1E 33
Limbrick Cnr. BN12: Gor S ...6E 19
Limbrick La. BN12: Gor S ...6E 19
   (not continuous)
Limbrick Way BN12: Gor S ...6D 18
Lime Rd. BN14: Fin ...2C 6
Limes, The *BN2: Brig* ...*2F 29*
   (off Bromley Rd.)
   BN14: Fin ...1C 6
Limney Rd. BN2: Brig ...3A 30
Lincett Av. BN13: Wor ...6H 19
Lincett Ct. BN13: Wor ...6H 19
Lincett Dr. BN13: Wor ...1H 33
Linchmere Rd. BN2: Brig ...3B 30
Linchmere Av. BN2: Salt ...3A 38
Lincoln Av. BN10: Peace ...5E 39
Lincoln Av. Sth. BN10: Peace ...5E 39
Lincoln Cotts. BN2: Brig ...4F 29
Lincoln Ct. BN3: Hove ...2A 28
   BN10: Peace ...5E 39
   BN15: Lan ...6C 22
Lincoln Rd. BN13: Wor ...6H 19
   BN41: Port ...3B 26
Lincoln St. BN2: Brig ...4F 29
Linden Lodge *BN11: Wor* ...*2C 34*
   (off Tennyson Rd.)
Lindens, The *BN2: Brig* ...*3F 29*
   (off Canterbury Dr.)
Lindfield *BN41: Port* ...*1B 26*
   (off Windlesham Cl.)
Lindfield Av. BN25: Sea ...5H 43
Lindfield Cl. BN2: Salt ...2H 37
Lindfield Ct. *BN1: Brig* ...*1G 29*
   (off The Crestway)
Lindum Rd. BN13: W Tar ...5H 19
Lindum Way BN13: Wor ...5H 19
Linemans Vw. *BN43: Shor S* ...*3A 24*
   (off Broad Reach)
Lingfield Cl. BN13: Salv ...4H 19
Link Pl. BN1: Brig ...1F 29
Links Av. BN10: Peace ...4C 40
Links Cl. BN25: Sea ...4F 43
   BN41: Port ...2C 26
Links Rd. BN14: Fin V ...2A 20
   BN15: Lan ...4D 22
   BN25: Sea ...5F 43
   BN41: Port ...2C 26
Linkway, The BN1: Brig ...1F 29
   BN11: Wor ...1C 34
Linthouse Cl. BN10: Peace ...2H 39
Linton Rd. BN3: Hove ...2F 27
Lion M. BN3: Hove ...3F 27
Lions Cl. BN2: Brig ...5A 30
Lions Dene BN1: Brig ...4B 12
Lions Gdns. BN1: Brig ...6B 12
Lions Ga. BN3: Hove ...1E 27
Lions Pl. BN25: Sea ...5E 43
Liphook Cl. BN1: Brig ...1G 29
Lisher Rd. BN15: Lan ...3D 22
Litlington Ct. BN25: Sea ...3B 42
Little Cres. BN2: Rott ...3G 37
Little Drove BN44: Bramb ...4C 4
Lit. East St.
   BN1: Brig ...6C **44** (6E **29**)
   BN7: Lew ...4F 17
Little Gables BN13: Durr ...4H 19
Lit. George St.
   BN2: Brig ...5D **44** (5E **29**)
Littlehampton Rd.
   BN12: Fer, Gor S ...1A 32
   BN13: Wor, Gor S, Salv ...1A 32
Little High St. BN11: Wor ...1D 34
   BN43: Shor S ...3A 24
Little Mead *BN12: Gor S* ...*2E 33*
   (off Marlborough Rd.)
Little Paddocks BN12: Fer ...3A 32
Lit. Paddocks Way BN12: Fer ...3B 32

Little Pembrokes BN11: Wor ...1A 34
Lit. Preston St. BN1: Brig ...5C 28
Littlestone Rd. BN13: Durr ...4G 19
Lit. Western St. BN3: Brig ...5B 28
Littleworth Cl. BN3: Hove ...3H 31
Liverpool Bldgs. *BN11: Wor* ...*2D 34*
   (off Liverpool Rd.)
Liverpool Gdns. BN11: Wor ...2D 34
Liverpool Rd. BN11: Wor ...2D 34
Liverpool Row BN11: Wor ...2D 34
Liverpool Ter. BN11: Wor ...2D 34
Livesay Cres. BN14: Broad ...6D 20
Livingstone Ho. BN3: Hove ...3H 27
Livingstone Rd. BN3: Hove ...3H 27
Livingstone St. BN2: Brig ...5H 29
Llandaff Ct. BN1: Wor ...2A 34
Lloyd Cl. BN3: Hove ...1A 28
Lloyd Rd. BN3: Hove ...2A 28
Locks Cl. BN42: S'wick ...3G 25
Locks Cres. BN41: Port ...2B 26
Locks Hill BN41: Port ...1B 26
Lockwood Cl. BN2: W'dean ...3G 31
Lockwood Cres. BN2: W'dean ...2G 31
Loddon Cl. BN13: Durr ...2E 19
Loder Gdns. BN14: Broad ...5C 20
Loder Pl. BN1: Brig ...6D 12
Loder Rd. BN1: Brig ...6D 12
Lodge, The BN2: Brig ...2F 29
Lodge Cl. BN7: Lew ...5C 16
   BN41: Port ...6H 9
Lodge Ct. BN43: Shor S ...1A 24
Lodsworth BN2: Brig ...2B 30
Lodsworth Cl. BN2: Brig ...3A 30
Lomond Av. BN1: Brig ...1F 13
London Rd. BN1: Brig ...1D **44** (3E **29**)
   (Baker St.)
   BN1: Brig ...4B 12
   (Coolwater Pk.)
   BN1: Brig ...1B 12
   (Mill Rd. Rdbt.)
London Road Station (Rail) ...2E 29
London St. BN11: Wor ...1C 34
London Ter. BN1: Brig ...1D **44** (3E **29**)
Loney Ct. BN43: Shor S ...2E 25
Longcroft BN3: Hove ...3A 24
Longfellow Rd. BN11: Wor ...1B 34
Longfurlong
   BN13: Clap, Fin, Pat
   ...2A **18** & 3A **6**
   BN14: Fin ...3A 6
Longhill Cl. BN2: O'dean ...6G 31
Longhill Rd. BN2: O'dean ...6F 31
Longlands BN14: Char D ...2D 20
Longlands Glade
   BN14: Char D ...2D 20
Longlands Spinney
   BN14: Char D ...2D 20
Longley Ind. Est. BN1: Brig ...3E 29
Long Meadow BN14: Fin V ...4D 6
Longridge Av. BN2: Salt ...4A 38
Looes Barn Cl. BN2: Salt ...1B 38
Loose La. BN15: Somp ...5G 21
Lords, The BN25: Sea ...1D 42
Loriners Ct. BN3: Hove ...2D 26
Lorna Rd. BN3: Hove ...3A 28
Lorne Rd. BN1: Brig ...2E 29
Lorne Vs. BN1: Brig ...6C 12
Lorraine Ct. *BN3: Hove* ...*3C 28*
   (off Davigdor Rd.)
   BN3: Hove ...4H 27
   (Parnell Ct.)
Lorraine Rd. BN9: New ...4F 41
Lotts La. BN15: Somp ...4A 22
Lovegrove Ct. BN3: Hove ...2E 27
Love La. BN7: Lew ...5C 16
Lover's Wlk. BN1: Brig ...2D 28
Lover's Wlk. Cotts. BN1: Brig ...2D 28
Lovett Cl. BN12: Gor S ...6E 19
Lwr. Beach Rd. BN43: Shor S ...4B 24
LOWER BEVENDEAN ...1A 30
Lwr. Bevendean Av. BN2: Brig ...1A 30
Lwr. Chalvington Pl.
   ...5A 30
LOWER COKEHAM ...5A 22
Lower Dr. BN25: Sea ...2E 43
   BN42: S'wick ...1G 25
Lwr. Market St. BN3: Hove ...5B 28
Lower Pl. BN9: New ...4E 41
Lwr. Rock Gdns. BN2: Brig ...6F 29
Lower St. BN13: Durr ...3H 19
Lowther Rd. BN1: Brig ...6E 13
   BN13: Durr ...3H 19
Loxley Gdns. BN14: Wor ...6C 20
Loxwood Av. BN14: Wor ...4B 20

Loyal Pde. BN1: Brig ...3A 12
Lucerne Cl. BN41: Port ...1B 26
Lucerne Rd. BN1: Brig ...1D 28
Lucinda Way BN25: Sea ...2E 43
Lucraft Rd. BN2: Brig ...3B 14
Ludlow Cl. BN11: Wor ...1F 35
Ludlow Ri. BN2: Brig ...1C 30
Lulham Cl. BN10: Tel C ...2F 39
Lullington Av. BN3: Hove ...2F 27
Lullington Cl. BN25: Sea ...5G 43
Lureland Ct. BN10: Peace ...6G 39
Lustrells Cl. BN2: Salt ...2H 37
Lustrells Cres. BN2: Salt ...2H 37
Lustrells Rd. BN2: Rott ...2G 37
Lustrells Va. BN2: Salt ...2H 37
Luther M. BN2: Brig ...3G 29
Luther St. BN2: Brig ...3G 29
Lychpole Wlk. BN12: Gor S ...6D 18
Lyminster Av. BN1: Brig ...4E 13
Lynchet Cl. BN1: Brig ...6G 13
Lynchet Down BN1: Brig ...6G 13
Lynchets, The BN7: Lew ...2G 17
Lynchets Cres. BN3: Hove ...5D 10
Lynchette, The BN43: Shor S ...1B 24
Lynchet Wlk. BN1: Brig ...6G 13
Lynchmere Av. BN15: N Lan ...2B 22
Lynden Ct. BN1: Brig ...6C 12
Lyndhurst Cnr. *BN3: Hove* ...*3B 28*
   (off Lyndhurst Rd.)
Lyndhurst Ct. BN3: Hove ...3B 28
Lyndhurst Rd. BN3: Hove ...3B 28
   BN11: Wor ...2E 35
Lyn Rd. BN13: Durr ...4E 19
Lynton St. BN2: Brig ...3G 29
Lynwood Rd. BN2: Salt ...4A 38
Lyon Cl. BN3: Hove ...3B 28
Lyons Farm Retail Pk.
   BN14: Char D ...3E 21
Lyons Way BN14: Char D ...2E 21

M

McKerchar Cl. BN15: Lan ...3D 22
Mackie Av. BN1: Brig ...2D 12
McNair Ct. BN3: Hove ...3E 27
McWilliam Rd. BN2: W'dean ...1F 31
Madehurst Cl. BN2: Brig ...5H 29
Madeira Av. BN11: Wor ...1E 35
Madeira Colonnade *BN2: Brig* ...*6F 29*
   (off Madeira Dr.)
Madeira Dr.
   BN2: Brig ...6D **44** (6F **29**)
Madeira Pl. BN2: Brig ...6F 29
Mafeking Rd. BN2: Brig ...1G 29
Magnolia Cl. BN13: Durr ...5D 18
Magnus Pl. *BN43: Shor S* ...*3A 24*
   (off Broad Reach)
Maines Farm Rd. BN44: Up B ...5G 5
Mainstone Rd. BN3: Hove ...3F 27
Major Cl. BN1: Brig ...1F 29
Malcolm Cl. BN12: Fer ...3A 32
Maldon Rd. BN1: Brig ...6B 12
Malines Av. BN10: Peace ...5E 39
Malines Av. Sth. BN10: Peace ...5E 39
Mallet Cl. BN25: Sea ...5D 42
Malling Cl. BN7: Lew ...2F 17
Malling Down BN7: Lew ...2G 17
Malling Down Nature Reserve
   ...3H 17
Malling Hill BN7: Lew ...2G 17
Malling Ind. Est. BN7: Lew ...3F 17
Malling St. BN7: Lew ...4G 17
Mallory Rd. BN3: Hove ...6A 12
Malthouse, The *BN7: Lew* ...*5E 17*
   (off Cluny St.)
Malthouse Cl. BN15: Somp ...3H 21
Malthouse Cotts. BN12: Gor S ...2E 33
Malthouse Ct. BN2: Brig ...5F 29
Malthouse La. BN2: Brig ...4F 29
Malthouse Trad. Est.
   BN43: Shor S ...3D 24
Maltings Barn, The *BN7: Lew* ...*4F 17*
   (off Foundry La.)
Maltings Grn. *BN44: Stey* ...*4C 4*
   (off Castle La.)
Malvern Cl. BN11: Wor ...1H 35
Malvern St. BN3: Hove ...3H 27
Manchester St.
   BN2: Brig ...6D **44** (6E **29**)
Mandalay Ct. BN1: Brig ...4B 12
Manhattan Ct. *BN1: Brig* ...*4B 12*
   (off Tongdean La.)
Manitoba Way BN13: Durr ...4E 19
Mannings BN43: Shor S ...3B 24

Manor, The—Millyard Cres.

Manor, The BN11: Wor . . . 2B 34
Manor Cl. BN2: Brig . . . 5A 30
BN11: Wor . . . 2B 34
BN15: Lan . . . 3D 22
BN25: Sea . . . 4G 43
BN42: S'wick . . . 2A 26
Manor Ct. BN11: Wor . . . 3B 34
BN15: N Lan . . . 2B 22
BN25: Sea . . . 4G 43
BN42: S'wick . . . 3A 26
Manor Cres. BN2: Brig . . . 5A 30
Manor Dr. BN10: Tel C . . . 3F 39
Manor Fld. Ct.
BN14: Broad . . . 5D 20
Manor Gdns. BN2: Brig . . . 5A 30
Manor Grn. BN2: Brig . . . 5A 30
Mnr. Hall Rd. BN42: S'wick . . . 2H 25
Manor Hill BN2: Brig . . . 4H 29
Manor Ho. BN11: Wor . . . 2B 34
BN15: N Lan . . . 2D 22
Manor Lea BN11: Wor . . . 3B 34
Manor Paddock BN2: Brig . . . 4A 36
Mnr. Paddock Ho. *BN2: Brig . . . 4A 36*
(off Manor Paddock)
Manor Pde. BN13: Durr . . . 3F 19
Manor Pk. BN15: Lan . . . 3D 22
Manor Pl. BN2: Brig . . . 4A 36
Manor Rd. BN2: Brig . . . 4A 36
BN11: Wor . . . 2B 34
BN15: N Lan . . . 2B 22
BN25: Sea . . . 4G 43
BN41: Port . . . 1B 26
BN44: Up B . . . 5G 5
Manor Rd. Nth. BN25: Sea . . . 3G 43
Manor Ter. *BN7: Lew . . . 5E 17*
(off The Course)
Manor Vw. Ct. BN14: Broad . . . 5D 20
Manor Way BN2: Brig . . . 5A 30
BN15: Lan . . . 3D 22
Mansell Rd. BN43: Shor S . . . 2D 24
Mansfield Cl. BN11: Wor . . . 6G 21
Mansfield Rd. BN3: Hove . . . 3E 27
BN11: Wor . . . 1G 35
Mantell Cl. BN7: Lew . . . 1E 17
Mantell Ho. *BN2: Brig . . . 5F 29*
(off Lennox St.)
Manton Rd. BN2: Brig . . . 1A 30
Mapel Flds. BN25: Sea . . . 1F 43
Maple Cl. BN2: W'dean . . . 3G 31
BN13: High S . . . 1G 19
Maple Ct. BN11: Wor . . . 2H 33
Maple Gdns. BN3: Hove . . . 1E 27
Maple Ho. *BN2: Brig . . . 2F 29*
(off Bromley Rd.)
BN12: Gor S . . . 6C 18
(off Goring Chase)
Maplehurst Rd. BN41: Port . . . 1A 26
Maple Leaf Cl. BN9: New . . . 4D 40
Maple Rd. BN10: Peace . . . 5B 40
Maples, The BN12: Fer . . . 4B 32
Maple Wlk. BN15: Somp . . . 3H 21
Maplewood *BN1: Brig . . . 5C 12*
(off Curwen Pl.)
March Ho. BN3: Hove . . . 1H 27
Mardale Rd. BN13: Durr . . . 4H 19
Marden Cl. BN2: W'dean . . . 1G 31
Mardyke BN43: Shor B . . . 4H 23
Maresfield Rd. BN2: Brig . . . 5A 30
Margaret Ct. BN10: Peace . . . 5F 39
Margaret St. BN2: Brig . . . 6F 29
Margery Rd. BN3: Hove . . . 2D 26
Marina Ct. BN15: S Lan . . . 5G 23
Marina Water Tours . . . *5B 36*
(off Village Sq.)
Marina Way BN2: Brig . . . 5B 36
Marine Av. BN3: Hove . . . 4E 27
Marine Cl. BN2: Salt . . . 3H 37
BN11: Wor . . . 3A 34
Marine Ct. *BN2: Rott . . . 3G 37*
(off Marine Dr.)
BN2: Salt . . . 4A 38
BN9: New . . . 5F 41
BN10: Tel C . . . 5D 38
BN25: Sea . . . 4B 42
(off Connaught Rd.)
BN43: Shor B . . . 4H 23
Marine Cres. BN12: Gor S . . . 4E 33
BN25: Sea . . . 5D 42
Marine Dr. BN2: Brig . . . 5B 36
BN2: O'dean, Rott, Salt . . . 3E 37
BN12: Gor S . . . 4C 32
BN25: Sea . . . 1A 42
Marine Gdns. . . . 3A 34
Marine Gdns. BN2: Brig . . . 6F 29
Marine Ga. BN2: Brig . . . 5B 36
Marine Pde. BN2: Brig . . . 6D 44 (6F 29)
BN11: Wor . . . 3C 34
BN25: Sea . . . 3A 42
Marine Path *BN2: Salt . . . 3A 38*
(off Marine Dr.)
Marine Pl. BN11: Wor . . . 2D 34
Marine Point BN11: Wor . . . 3A 34
Mariners, The BN15: Lan . . . 6A 22
Mariners Cl. BN43: Shor B . . . 5H 23
Mariner's Quay BN2: Brig . . . 5B 36
Mariners Wharf BN9: New . . . 6F 41
Marine Sq. BN2: Brig . . . 6G 29
Marine Ter. M. *BN2: Brig . . . 6G 29*
(off Bristol Rd.)
Marine Vw. BN2: Brig . . . 5F 29
BN9: New . . . 5D 40
(not continuous)
Marjoram Pl. BN43: Shor S . . . 1D 24
Mark Cl. BN25: Sea . . . 5H 43
Market Fld. BN44: Stey . . . 3D 4
Market La. BN7: Lew . . . 4F 17
Market Pl. BN13: W Tar . . . 5A 20
Market St. BN1: Brig . . . 5C 44 (5E 29)
BN7: Lew . . . 4F 17
BN11: Wor . . . 2D 34
Markwick M. BN11: Wor . . . 1E 35
Marlborough Bus. Cen.
BN15: Lan . . . 6A 22
Marlborough Ct. BN3: Hove . . . 3A 28
BN9: New . . . 4E 41
(off Church Hill)
Marlborough M.
BN1: Brig . . . 4A 44 (5D 28)
Marlborough Pl. BN1: Brig . . . 3D 44
(Blenheim Pl.)
BN1: Brig . . . 4D 44 (5E 29)
(Grand Pde.)
Marlborough Rd. BN12: Gor S . . . 2E 33
BN15: Lan . . . 6A 22
Marlborough St.
BN1: Brig . . . 4A 44 (5D 28)
Marlborough Way
BN12: Gor S . . . 2F 33
Marlin Ct. BN15: S Lan . . . 6C 22
Marline Ct. BN43: Shor S . . . 3A 24
Marlinespike, The
BN43: Shor B . . . 4C 24
Marlipins Mus. . . . 3A 24
Marlow Ct. BN2: Brig . . . 3F 29
Marlowe Rd. BN14: Broad . . . 5E 21
Marlow Rd. BN2: Brig . . . 4B 36
Marmion Rd. BN3: Hove . . . 3F 27
Marsden Ct. BN10: Tel C . . . 5E 39
Marshall Av. BN14: Fin V . . . 5D 6
Marshall La. BN9: New . . . 4E 41
Marshalls Row
BN1: Brig . . . 1D 44 (3E 29)
Marshall Way BN3: Hove . . . 1F 27
Marsh Ho. BN42: S'wick . . . 3F 25
Marston Ct. *BN3: Hove . . . 3C 28*
(off Davigdor Rd.)
Marston Rd. BN14: Broad . . . 6E 21
Martello Ct. BN9: New . . . 2F 41
Martello M. BN25: Sea . . . 5D 42
Martello Rd. BN25: Sea . . . 5D 42
Martha Gunn Rd. BN2: Brig . . . 1A 30
Martin Rd. BN3: Hove . . . 1D 26
Martins, The BN10: Tel C . . . 2F 39
Martlet, The BN3: Hove . . . 2B 28
Martlet Ct. *BN2: Brig . . . 5G 29*
(off Hereford St.)
Martlet Ho. BN1: Brig . . . 2E 29
BN2: Salt . . . 4B 38
Martlets, The BN15: Somp . . . 4A 22
BN43: Shor S . . . 2B 24
MARTLETS HOSPICE . . . 1F 27
Martlets Trad. Est.
BN12: Gor S . . . 1E 33
Martlets Way BN12: Gor S . . . 1E 33
Martletts, The BN7: Lew . . . 2F 17
Martyns Cl. BN2: O'dean . . . 6G 31
Mash Barn La. BN15: Lan . . . 2E 23
Mason Rd. BN25: Sea . . . 3E 43
Matlock Rd. BN1: Brig . . . 1B 28
Matthew Ho. *BN3: Hove . . . 4G 27*
(off Miles Wlk.)
Maudlin La. BN44: Bramb . . . 4C 4
Maudlyn Cl. BN44: Bramb . . . 5D 4
Maudlyn Pk. BN44: Bramb . . . 5C 4
Maudlyn Parkway
BN44: Bramb . . . 5C 4
Maurice Rd. BN25: Sea . . . 6E 43
Max Millers Wlk. BN2: Brig . . . 6F 29
May Av. BN25: Sea . . . 4G 43
Maybridge Cres. BN12: Gor S . . . 1E 33
Maybridge Sq. BN12: Gor S . . . 6E 19
May Cl. BN12: Gor S . . . 6E 19
May Cotts. BN2: Brig . . . 2G 29
Mayfield Av. BN10: Peace . . . 6H 39
(not continuous)
Mayfield Cl. BN1: Brig . . . 3D 12
BN14: Fin V . . . 1A 20
Mayfield Ct. BN2: Salt . . . 2A 38
Mayfield Cres. BN1: Brig . . . 3D 12
Mayflower Ct. *BN43: Shor B . . . 4C 24*
(off Emerald Quay)
Mayflower Sq.
BN1: Brig . . . 1C 44 (3E 29)
Mayhew Way BN7: Lew . . . 3F 17
Mayo Ct. BN2: Brig . . . 2F 29
Mayo Rd. BN2: Brig . . . 2F 29
May Rd. BN2: Brig . . . 3H 29
Maytree Av. BN14: Fin V . . . 4D 6
Maytree Cl. *BN3: Hove . . . 2D 26*
(off Dorothy Rd.)
BN15: Somp . . . 4H 21
Maytree Wlk. BN3: Hove . . . 1E 27
Meadow Cl. BN2: Rott . . . 1E 37
BN3: Hove . . . 5H 11
BN11: Wor . . . 1H 35
BN41: Port . . . 6B 10
BN42: S'wick . . . 2H 25
Meadow Ct. Est. BN11: Wor . . . 1H 35
Meadow Cres. BN11: Wor . . . 1G 35
MEADOWFIELD . . . 2F 19
Meadow La. BN15: Lan . . . 5C 22
Meadow Pde. BN2: Rott . . . 1F 37
Meadow Rd. BN11: Wor . . . 1G 35
Meadow Rd. Ind. Est.
BN11: Wor . . . 6H 21
Meadows, The BN3: Hove . . . 5D 10
BN7: Lew . . . 2G 17
Meadowside Ct. BN12: Gor S . . . 2C 32
Meadow Sweet Cl.
BN13: Durr . . . 5C 18
Meadowview BN2: Brig . . . 1A 30
Meadowview Rd.
BN15: Somp . . . 2A 22
Meadow Way BN12: Fer . . . 2A 32
BN25: Sea . . . 4G 43
Meads, The BN1: Brig . . . 3H 13
Meads Av. BN3: Hove . . . 5C 10
Meads Cl. BN3: Hove . . . 5C 10
Meads Rd. BN25: Sea . . . 4E 43
Meadway, The BN2: Brig . . . 5B 30
BN43: Shor B . . . 4B 24
Meadway Ct. BN13: Wor . . . 6G 19
BN42: S'wick . . . 2F 25
Meadway Cres. BN3: Hove . . . 6F 11
Mealla Cl. BN7: Lew . . . 2E 17
Measham Cl. BN12: Fer . . . 3B 32
Medina Pl. BN3: Hove . . . 4H 27
Medina Ter. BN3: Hove . . . 5H 27
Medina Vs. BN3: Hove . . . 4H 27
Medmerry Hill BN2: Brig . . . 6A 14
Medway Cl. BN13: Durr . . . 3F 19
Medway Ct. *BN2: Brig . . . 5F 29*
(off Carlton Hill)
Meeching Ct. BN9: New . . . 4F 41
Meeching Pl. BN9: New . . . 4E 41
Meeching Ri. BN9: New . . . 4E 41
Meeching Rd. BN9: New . . . 4F 41
Meeting Ho. La. BN1: Brig . . . 5C 44
Melbourne Av. BN12: Gor S . . . 2E 33
Melbourne Rd. BN12: Gor S . . . 2F 33
Melbourne St. BN2: Brig . . . 2G 29
Melbourne Way BN12: Gor S . . . 2E 33
Melrose Av. BN13: Wor . . . 6G 19
BN41: Port . . . 1A 26
Melrose Cl. BN1: Brig . . . 6G 13
BN13: Wor . . . 6G 19
Melville Rd.
BN3: Hove . . . 1A 44 (3C 28)
Melville Way BN12: Gor S . . . 6E 19
Mendip Cres. BN13: Durr . . . 3G 19
Mendip Rd. BN13: Durr . . . 3G 19
Mercread Rd. BN25: Sea . . . 4E 43
Meredith Rd. BN14: Broad . . . 6F 21
Merevale BN1: Brig . . . 6F 13
Meridian Cen. BN10: Peace . . . 4G 39
Meridian Ind. Est., The
BN10: Peace . . . 5G 39
Meridian Monument . . . 6F 39
Meridian Rd. BN7: Lew . . . 3D 16
Meridian Way BN10: Peace . . . 5G 39
Merlin Cl. BN3: Hove . . . 2B 28
Merlin Ct. BN13: Salv . . . 4H 19
Merryfield Ct. *BN25: Sea . . . 4B 42*
(off Marine Pde.)
Mersey Cl. BN13: Durr . . . 3E 19
Mersey Rd. BN13: Durr . . . 3E 19
Mersham Gdns. BN12: Gor S . . . 2E 33
Merston Cl. BN2: W'dean . . . 4G 31
Merton Ct. BN2: Brig . . . 1A 36
Merton Rd. BN11: Wor . . . 2F 35
Merton Ter. BN11: Wor . . . 2F 35
Metcalfe Av. BN9: New . . . 3D 40
Metropole Ct. BN1: Brig . . . 5A 44
Mews, The *BN1: Brig . . . 6C 12*
(off Towergate)
BN11: Wor . . . 2C 34
(off Shakespeare Rd.)
BN25: Sea . . . 3G 43
Mews Cotts., The BN3: Hove . . . 6G 11
Meyners Cl. BN3: Hove . . . 5C 10
Micklefield Way BN25: Sea . . . 4G 43
Middle Furlong BN25: Sea . . . 4E 43
Middle Mead BN44: Stey . . . 2C 4
Middle Onslow Cl. BN12: Fer . . . 1A 32
Middle Rd. BN1: Brig . . . 1C 28
BN15: Lan . . . 5B 22
BN43: Shor S . . . 2C 24
Middle St. BN1: Brig . . . 5B 44 (5D 28)
BN1: Falm . . . 2E 15
BN41: Port . . . 4B 26
BN43: Shor S . . . 3B 24
Middleton Av. BN3: Hove . . . 4D 26
Middleton Ri. BN1: Brig . . . 3A 14
Middle Tyne BN13: Durr . . . 5F 19
Middle Way BN7: Lew . . . 4C 16
BN16: King G . . . 4A 32
Midhurst Cl. BN12: Fer . . . 2B 32
Midhurst Dr. BN12: Fer . . . 2B 32
Midhurst Ri. BN1: Brig . . . 2F 13
Midhurst Wlk. BN3: Hove . . . 5F 11
Midway Rd. BN2: W'dean . . . 2E 31
Mighell St. BN2: Brig . . . 5F 29
Milbanke's Wlk. BN1: Stan . . . 1H 13
Milbury Cl. BN12: Fer . . . 4B 32
Milcote Av. BN3: Hove . . . 2F 27
Mildmay Rd. BN7: Lew . . . 4C 16
Mile End Cotts. BN1: Brig . . . 2C 12
MILE OAK . . . 5H 9
Mile Oak Cres. BN42: S'wick . . . 1H 25
Mile Oak Gdns. BN41: Port . . . 1A 26
Mile Oak Rd. BN41: Port . . . 4G 9
BN42: S'wick . . . 1H 25
Miles Ct. *BN2: Brig . . . 5G 29*
(off Hereford St.)
Miles Wlk. BN3: Hove . . . 4H 27
Milford Ct. BN15: Lan . . . 6B 22
Mill Av. BN43: Shor S . . . 1B 24
Millberg Rd. BN25: Sea . . . 3G 43
Mill Cl. BN41: Port . . . 1C 26
Mill Ct. BN11: Wor . . . 2B 34
Millcroft BN1: Brig . . . 3A 12
Millcroft Av. BN42: S'wick . . . 1G 25
Millcroft Gdns. BN42: S'wick . . . 1G 25
Millcross Rd. BN41: Port . . . 1B 26
Milldown Rd. BN25: Sea . . . 3E 43
Mill Dr. BN3: Hove . . . 5G 11
BN25: Sea . . . 4E 43
Mill Drove
BN25: Sea . . . 6H 41 & 2A 42
Millennium Cl. BN15: S Lan . . . 4F 23
Miller Pl. BN41: Port . . . 5A 10
Millers Rd. BN1: Brig . . . 1C 28
Millfield BN15: Somp . . . 3A 22
BN44: Bramb . . . 4F 5
Millfield Cl. BN25: Sea . . . 3F 43
Millfield Cotts. BN2: Brig . . . 6H 29
MILL HILL . . . 1A 24
Mill Hill BN43: Shor S . . . 3A 8
Mill Hill Cl. BN43: Shor S . . . 1A 24
Mill Hill Dr. BN43: Shor S . . . 1A 24
Mill Hill Gdns. BN43: Shor S . . . 1A 24
Mill Hill Nature Reserve . . . 5A 8
Mill Ho. BN11: Wor . . . 1H 35
Mill Ho. Gdns. BN11: Wor . . . 2A 34
Mill La. BN13: High S . . . 6C 6
BN41: Port . . . 6B 10
BN43: Shor S . . . 2A 24
Mill Ri. BN1: Brig . . . 3A 12
Mill Rd. BN1: Brig . . . 3H 11
BN7: Lew . . . 2G 17
BN11: Wor . . . 2H 33
BN15: N Lan . . . 1C 22
BN41: Port . . . 3B 26
BN44: Stey . . . 3B 4
Mill Rd. Ind. Est. BN41: Port . . . 3B 26
Mill Rd. Rdbt. BN1: Brig . . . 1B 12
Mill Row BN1: Brig . . . 2A 44
Mill St. BN1: Falm . . . 1E 15
MILL VIEW HOSPITAL . . . 1E 27
Millyard Cres. BN2: W'dean . . . 3F 31

Raglan Ct.—Ryecroft

Raglan Ct. *BN1: Brig* 4B **44**
(off Portland St.)
BN11: Wor 2A **34**
Railway App. BN9: New 4F **41**
BN11: Wor 1C **34**
Railway La. BN7: Lew 4F **17**
Railway Rd. BN9: New 4F **41**
Railway St.
BN1: Brig 2B **44** (4D **28**)
Raleigh Cl. BN43: Shor B 4A **24**
Raleigh Cres. BN12: Gor S 1F **33**
Raleigh Way BN12: Gor S 6E **19**
Ranalah Est. BN9: New 3F **41**
Ranelagh Vs. BN3: Hove 2H **27**
Ranscombe Hill BN8: Glyn 6H **17**
Raphael Rd. BN3: Hove 3F **27**
Ravensbourne Av.
BN43: Shor S 1B **24**
Ravensbourne Cl.
BN43: Shor S 1B **24**
Raven's Rd. BN43: Shor S 3B **24**
Ravenswood Ct.
BN13: W Tar 5H **19**
Ravenswood Dr. BN2: W'dean 4H **31**
Rayford Cl. BN10: Peace 5G **39**
Rayford Ct. *BN25: Sea* 5D **42**
(off St John's Rd.)
Raymond Cl. BN25: Sea 2F **43**
Reading Rd. BN2: Brig 4B **36**
Read's Wlk. BN44: Stey 1C **4**
Reba Ct. BN2: Salt 4B **38**
Rectory Cl. BN3: Hove 3D **26**
BN9: New 5E **41**
BN43: Shor S 3F **25**
Rectory Ct. *BN43: Shor S* 2E **25**
(off Pebble Way)
Rectory Farm Rd.
BN15: Somp 3H **21**
Rectory Gdns. BN14: Broad 4C **20**
Rectory La. BN13: Clap 1A **18**
Rectory Rd. BN9: New 1G **41**
BN14: W Tar 6A **20**
BN43: Shor S 3E **25**
Rectory Wlk. BN15: Somp 3A **22**
Redcotts BN11: Wor 1B **34**
Redhill Cl. BN1: Brig 3A **12**
Redhill Dr. BN1: Brig 3A **12**
Redvers Rd. BN2: Brig 1H **29**
Redwood Cl. BN13: Durr 5E **19**
Reed Ct. BN7: Lew 2E **17**
Rees Cl. BN13: Durr 4D **18**
Reeves Hill BN1: Brig 3H **13**
Refectory Rd. BN1: Falm 1D **14**
Regency Ct. BN1: Brig 5B **12**
BN12: Fer 2B **32**
BN13: Salv 4A **20**
Regency M.
BN1: Brig 4A **44** (5C **28**)
Regency Rd.
BN1: Brig 5A **44** (5D **28**)
(not continuous)
Regency Sq.
BN1: Brig 4A **44** (5C **28**)
Regency Town House 5B **28**
Regent Arc. BN1: Brig 5C **44**
Regent Cl. BN15: S Lan 4F **23**
Regent Hill
BN1: Brig 4A **44** (5D **28**)
Regent Row
BN1: Brig 4A **44** (5D **28**)
Regents Cl. BN25: Sea 2D **42**
Regent St. BN1: Brig 4C **44** (5E **29**)
Regis Ct. BN11: Wor 3A **34**
Reigate Ct. *BN11: Wor* 2H **33**
(off Reigate Rd.)
Reigate Rd. BN1: Brig 1B **28**
BN11: Wor 2H **33**
Reynolds Rd. BN3: Hove 3F **27**
Richard Allen Ct. BN1: Brig 1G **29**
Richardson Ct. BN3: Hove 3F **27**
Richardson Rd. BN3: Hove 3F **27**
Rich Ind. Est. BN9: New 2G **41**
Richington Way BN25: Sea 3G **43**
Richmond Ct. *BN3: Hove* 3C **28**
(off Osmond Rd.)
BN11: Wor 2C **34**
BN25: Sea 4D **42**
(off Richmond Rd.)
Richmond Gdns. BN2: Brig 4F **29**
Richmond Hgts. BN2: Brig 4F **29**
Richmond M. *BN25: Sea* 4D **42**
(off Richmond Rd.)
Richmond Pde. BN2: Brig 4E **29**
Richmond Pl.
BN2: Brig 2D **44** (4E **29**)
Richmond Rd. BN2: Brig 2F **29**
BN11: Wor 2C **34**
BN25: Sea 4D **42**
Richmond St. BN2: Brig 4F **29**
Richmond Ter. *BN2: Brig* 3F **29**
(off Lewes Rd.)
BN25: Sea 4D **42**
Ride, The BN1: Brig 1D **28**
Ridge Cl. BN41: Port 4A **10**
Ridge Rd. BN1: Falm 1E **15**
Ridgeside Av. BN1: Brig 3C **12**
Ridge Vw. BN1: Brig 3A **14**
Ridgeway BN42: S'wick 1H **25**
Ridgeway, The BN25: Sea 2E **43**
Ridgeway Cl. BN42: S'wick 1H **25**
Ridgeway Gdns. BN2: W'dean 3G **31**
Ridgewood Av. BN2: Salt 1A **38**
Ridgway, The BN2: W'dean 2F **31**
Ridgway Cl. BN2: W'dean 2F **31**
Ridings, The BN2: O'dean 6F **31**
BN10: Tel C 3F **39**
BN25: Sea 2E **43**
BN44: Bramb 5C **4**
Rifeside Gdns. BN12: Fer 1A **32**
Rife Way BN12: Fer 2A **32**
Rigden Rd. BN3: Hove 2A **28**
Riley Rd. BN2: Brig 2G **29**
Ringmer Cl. BN1: Brig 4A **14**
Ringmer Dr. BN1: Brig 4B **14**
Ringmer Rd. BN1: Brig 4A **14**
BN9: New 5C **40**
BN13: Wor 5G **19**
BN25: Sea 5D **42**
Ring Rd. BN15: N Lan 1C **22**
Ripley Rd. BN11: Wor 2H **33**
Ripon Ct. *BN11: Wor* 2A **34**
(off Pevensey Gdns.)
Rise, The BN41: Port 6H **9**
Risings, The BN25: Sea 3E **43**
Rissom Ct. BN1: Brig 6C **12**
Riverbank Bus. Cen.
BN43: Shor S 3A **24**
River Cl. BN43: Shor B 4A **24**
Riverdale BN7: Lew 3E **17**
Riverside BN9: New 4F **41**
BN42: S'wick 4G **25**
BN43: Shor B 4B **24**
BN44: Up B 4F **5**
Riverside Bus. Cen.
BN7: Lew 3F **17**
BN43: Shor S 3B **24**
Riverside Cvn. Pk.
BN44: Up B 4F **5**
Riverside Ct. *BN9: New* 4E **41**
(off North La.)
Riverside Ho. BN9: New 5F **41**
Riverside Ind. Est. BN7: Lew 3F **17**
Riverside Nth. BN9: New 4F **41**
Riverside Rd. BN43: Shor B 4B **24**
Riverside Sth. BN9: New 5F **41**
RNLI Lifeboat Station
Brighton **6B 36**
Newhaven **5F 41**
Shoreham **4E 25**
Robert Lodge BN2: Brig 4B **36**
Roberts Marine Mans.
BN11: Wor 4H **33**
(off West Pde.)
Robertson Rd. BN1: Brig 6B **12**
Roberts Rd. BN15: S Lan 6C **22**
Robert St. BN1: Brig 3C **44** (4E **29**)
Robin Davis Cl.
BN2: Brig 2A **30**
Robin Dene BN2: Brig 4A **36**
Robinia Lodge BN1: Brig 6C **12**
Robinson Cl. BN15: Lan 4C **22**
Robinson Rd. BN9: New 3E **41**
Robins Row BN41: Port 1A **26**
Robson Ct. BN12: Gor S 1G **33**
Robson Rd. BN12: Gor S 2G **33**
Rochester Cl. BN3: Hove 4B **28**
BN13: Durr 5D **18**
Rochester Ct. *BN3: Hove* 4B **28**
(off Rochester Gdns.)
BN11: Wor 2A **34**
(off Pevensey Gdns.)
Rochester Gdns. BN3: Hove 4B **28**
Rochester St. BN2: Brig 5H **29**
Rochford Way BN25: Sea 1A **42**
Rock Cl. *BN42: S'wick* 3G **25**
(off Whiterock Pl.)
Rock Gro. BN2: Brig 6H **29**
Rockingham Cl. BN13: Durr 4G **19**
Rockingham Ct. BN13: Durr 4G **19**
Rock Pl. BN2: Brig 6F **29**
Rock St. BN2: Brig 4A **36**
Roderick Av. BN10: Peace 6F **39**
(not continuous)
Roderick Av. Nth.
BN10: Peace 1G **39**
Roderick Ct. *BN10: Peace* 4G **39**
(off Roderick Av.)
Rodmell Av. BN2: Salt 3B **38**
Rodmell Ct. BN25: Sea 3B **42**
Rodmell Pl. BN1: Brig 2E **13**
Rodmell Rd. BN13: Wor 5G **19**
BN25: Sea 5G **43**
Roedale Rd. BN1: Brig 1F **29**
ROEDEAN **1B 36**
Roedean Cl. BN25: Sea 3F **43**
Roedean Ct. BN2: Brig 4B **36**
Roedean Cres. BN2: Brig 4C **36**
Roedean Hgts. BN2: Brig 4C **36**
Roedean Path BN2: Brig 1B **36**
Roedean Rd. BN2: Brig 4B **36**
BN13: Durr 4G **19**
Roedean Ter. BN2: Brig 1B **36**
Roedean Va. BN2: Brig 1B **36**
Roedean Way BN2: Brig 1A **36**
Rogate Cl. BN13: Salv 4A **20**
BN15: Somp 3H **21**
Rogate Rd. BN13: Salv 4H **19**
Roger's La. BN14: Fin 3C **6**
Roman Cl. BN25: Sea 1A **42**
Roman Cres. BN42: S'wick 2G **25**
Roman Rd. BN3: Hove 4D **26**
BN42: S'wick 2G **25**
BN44: Stey 4D **4**
Roman Wlk. BN15: Somp 3H **21**
Roman Way BN42: S'wick 2G **25**
Romany Cl. BN41: Port 2B **26**
Romany Rd. BN13: Durr 5D **18**
Romney Cl. BN25: Sea 4H **43**
Romney Ct. BN11: Wor 3H **33**
Romney Rd. BN2: Rott 3G **37**
BN11: Wor 3H **33**
Romsey Cl. BN1: Brig 6F **13**
Ronuk Ho. *BN41: Port* 2C **26**
(off Carlton Ter.)
Rookery Cl. BN1: Brig 1C **28**
BN9: New 1G **41**
ROOKERY HILL **1A 42**
Rookery Way BN9: New 1H **41**
BN25: Sea 2A **42**
Ropes Pas. *BN7: Lew* 4E **17**
(off High St.)
Ropetackle BN43: Shor S 3A **24**
Rope Wlk. BN43: Shor S 3A **24**
Rosebery Av. BN2: W'dean 2E **31**
BN12: Gor S 2G **33**
Rose Ct. BN11: Wor 1H **35**
Rosecroft Cl. BN15: Lan 5C **22**
Rosedene Cl. BN2: W'dean 4G **31**
Rose Hill BN2: Brig 3F **29**
Rose Hill Cl. BN1: Brig 3E **29**
Rose Hill Ct. *BN1: Brig* 3E **29**
(off Rose Hill Cl.)
Rose Hill Ter. BN1: Brig 3E **29**
Rosehill Ter. M. *BN1: Brig* 3E **29**
(off Rosehill Ter.)
Rosemary Av. BN44: Stey 3D **4**
Rosemary Cl. BN10: Peace 3G **39**
BN44: Stey 3D **4**
Rosemary Dr. BN43: Shor S 1D **24**
Rosemount Cl. BN25: Sea 1A **42**
Rose Wlk. BN12: Gor S 2G **33**
BN25: Sea 3E **43**
Rose Wlk., The BN9: New 4E **41**
(not continuous)
Rose Wlk. Cl. BN9: New 4D **40**
Rossiter Rd. BN15: N Lan 2C **22**
Rosslyn Av. BN43: Shor S 3C **24**
Rosslyn Ct. BN43: Shor S 2B **24**
Rosslyn Rd. BN43: Shor S 3B **24**
Rotary Ho. BN15: S Lan 6C **22**
Rotary Lodge BN1: Brig 2A **14**
BN11: Wor 1B **34**
Rotary Point BN41: Port 1A **26**
Rothbury Rd. BN3: Hove 3D **26**
Rotherfield Cl. BN1: Brig 2F **13**
Rotherfield Cres.
BN1: Brig 3F **13**
Rother Rd. BN25: Sea 5F **43**
Rothesay Cl. BN13: Wor 6G **19**
Rothwell Ct. BN9: New 4C **40**
Rotten Row BN7: Lew 5D **16**
ROTTINGDEAN **3F 37**
Rottingdean Pl. BN2: Rott 6H **31**
Rotyngs, The BN2: Rott 2F **37**
Rough Brow BN25: Sea 3F **43**
Roundhay Av. BN10: Peace 5A **40**
ROUND HILL **2F 29**
Roundhill Cres. BN2: Brig 2F **29**
Round Hill Rd. BN2: Brig 2F **29**
Round Hill St. BN2: Brig 2F **29**
Roundhouse Cres.
BN10: Peace 5H **39**
Roundway BN1: Brig 3A **14**
Roundwood BN13: High S 2H **19**
Rowan Av. BN3: Hove 1E **27**
Rowan Cl. BN25: Sea 4H **43**
BN41: Port 1A **26**
Rowan Ho. *BN2: Brig* 3F **29**
(off Canterbury Dr.)
BN12: Gor S 6C **18**
(off Goring Chase)
Rowans, The BN11: Wor 2A **34**
Rowans Ct. BN7: Lew 4E **17**
Rowan Way BN2: Rott 6G **31**
Rowe Av. BN10: Peace 6F **39**
(not continuous)
Rowe Av. Nth. BN10: Peace 4F **39**
Rowenden Ct. BN2: Salt 3A **38**
Rowlands Rd. BN11: Wor 3A **34**
Roxburgh Cl. BN13: Durr 3H **19**
ROYAL ALEXANDRA
CHILDREN'S HOSPITAL ***6H 29***
(within Royal Sussex County Hospital)
Royal Arc. *BN11: Wor* 3D **34**
(off South St.)
Royal Bldgs. BN15: Lan 6A **22**
Royal Cres. BN2: Brig 6G **29**
Royal Cres. Mans.
BN2: Brig 6G **29**
(off Marine Pde.)
Royal Cres. M. BN2: Brig 6G **29**
Royal Dr. BN25: Sea 1D **42**
Royal George Pde.
BN43: Shor S 1E **25**
Royal Pavilion, The **5D 44 (5E 29)**
ROYAL SUSSEX COUNTY HOSPITAL
6H 29
Royal Sussex Ct. BN7: Lew 5F **17**
Royles Cl. BN2: Rott 2G **37**
Rudd Ho. BN13: Durr 3G **19**
Rudgwick Av. BN12: Gor S 2C **32**
Rudyard Cl. BN2: W'dean 2G **31**
Rudyard Rd. BN2: W'dean 2G **31**
Rufus Cl. BN7: Lew 4E **17**
Rugby Cl. BN25: Sea 3G **43**
Rugby Ct. BN2: Brig 4A **36**
BN11: Wor 1A **34**
(off Rugby Rd.)
Rugby Pl. BN2: Brig 4A **36**
Rugby Rd. BN1: Brig 1E **29**
BN11: Wor 1H **33**
Rusbridge La. BN7: Lew 4G **17**
Rushey Hill Cvn. Pk.
BN10: Peace 5B **40**
Rushlake Cl. BN1: Brig 3A **14**
Rushlake Rd. BN1: Brig 2A **14**
Ruskin Pl. BN3: Hove 2F **27**
Ruskin Rd. BN3: Hove 2F **27**
BN14: Broad 6F **21**
Rusper Rd. BN1: Brig 2H **13**
BN13: Wor 5G **19**
Rusper Rd. Sth. BN13: Wor 5H **19**
Russell Cl. BN14: Broad 5E **21**
Russell Ct. BN15: S Lan 5C **22**
Russell Cres.
BN1: Brig 1A **44** (3C **28**)
Russell M. BN1: Brig 4A **44**
Russell Pl.
BN1: Brig 5A **44** (5D **28**)
Russell Rd.
BN1: Brig 5A **44** (5D **28**)
Russell Row BN7: Lew 2E **17**
Russells Dr. BN15: S Lan 5C **22**
Russell Sq.
BN1: Brig 4A **44** (5D **28**)
Rustic Cl. BN10: Peace 3F **39**
Rustic Pk. *BN10: Tel C* 2F **39**
(off Rustic Rd.)
Rustic Rd. BN10: Peace 2F **39**
Rustington Rd. BN1: Brig 3E **13**
Rutland Ct. BN3: Hove 3F **27**
Rutland Gdns. BN3: Hove 4F **27**
Rutland Rd. BN3: Hove 3G **27**
Ryde Ct. *BN3: Hove* 1D **26**
(off Hangleton Gdns.)
Ryde Rd. BN2: Brig 3H **29**
Rye Cl. BN2: Salt 2C **38**
BN11: Wor 3A **34**
BN25: Sea 3H **43**
Ryecroft BN2: Brig 5B **30**

Selborne Rd.—Stanmer Ct.

Selborne Rd. BN3: Hove 4A 28
BN11: Wor 1F 35
Selden La. BN11: Wor 2F 35
Selden Pde. BN13: Salv 3H 19
(off Salvington Rd.)
Selden Rd. BN11: Wor 1F 35
Seldens M. BN13: Salv 4H 19
Selden's Way BN13: Salv 4H 19
Sele Gdns. BN44: Up B 4G 5
Selham Cl. BN1: Brig 2A 14
Selham Dr. BN1: Brig 2H 13
Selham Pl. BN1: Brig 2H 13
(off Beatty Av.)
Selhurst Rd. BN2: W'dean 4G 31
Selkirk Cl. BN13: Wor 6G 19
Selmeston Ct. BN25: Sea 3B 42
Selmeston Pl. BN2: Brig 4B 30
Selsey Cl. BN1: Brig 2A 14
BN13: Wor 5H 19
Selsfield Dr. BN2: Brig 5H 13
Semley Rd. BN1: Brig 1E 29
Senlac Rd. BN9: New 4F 41
Sett, The BN41: Port 6B 10
Sevelands Cl. BN2: Brig 3B 30
Seven Dials BN1: Brig . . .1A 44 (3D 28)
Seventh Av. BN15: N Lan 2C 22
Severn Lodge BN2: Brig 5F 29
(off Mt. Pleasant)
Seville St. BN2: Brig 3G 29
Seymour Ho. BN2: Brig 6H 29
(off Seymour St.)
Seymour Sq. BN2: Brig 6H 29
Seymour St. BN2: Brig 6H 29
Shadwells Cl. BN15: Lan 3D 22
Shadwells Ct. BN15: Lan 3D 22
Shadwells Rd. BN15: Lan 3D 22
Shaftesbury Av. BN12: Gor S . . .1G 33
Shaftesbury Pl. BN1: Brig 2E 29
Shaftesbury Rd. BN1: Brig 2E 29
Shakespeare Rd. BN11: Wor 1B 34
Shakespeare St. BN3: Hove 2G 27
Shandon Gdns. BN14: Broad 4D 20
Shandon Rd. BN14: Broad 3D 20
Shandon Way BN14: Broad 4D 20
Shanklin Ct. BN2: Brig 2G 29
BN3: Hove 1D 26
(off Hangleton Rd.)
Shanklin Rd. BN2: Brig 2G 29
Shannon Cl. BN10: Tel C 3E 39
Sharpthorne Ct. BN1: Brig 1C 44
Sharpthorne Cres. BN41: Port . . .6C 10
Shawcross Ho. BN1: Brig 6C 12
Sheepbell Cl. BN41: Port 5B 10
Sheepcote Valley Camping & Cvn. Site
BN2: Brig 5C 30
Sheepfair BN7: Lew 3C 16
Sheepfold, The BN10: Peace 3G 39
Sheep Pen La. BN25: Sea 4F 43
BN44: Stey 3C 4
Sheep Wlk. BN2: Rott 1E 37
Sheffield Ct. BN1: Brig 1C 44
Shelby Rd. BN13: Durr 4E 19
Sheldon Ct. BN11: Wor 3B 34
Shelldale Av. BN41: Port 3B 26
Shelldale Cres. BN41: Port 3B 26
Shelldale Rd. BN41: Port 2B 26
Shelley Cl. BN7: Lew 4D 16
Shelley Ct. BN11: Wor 2C 34
Shelley Rd. BN3: Hove 3F 27
BN11: Wor 2B 34
Shenfield Way BN1: Brig 5F 13
Shepham Av. BN2: Salt 3A 38
Shepherd Ind. Est. BN7: Lew 3F 17
Shepherds Cl. BN9: Pidd 1D 40
Shepherds Cot BN10: Peace 2H 39
Shepherds Cft. BN1: Brig 4A 12
BN14: Fin 2C 6
(off Southview Rd.)
Shepherd's Mead BN14: Fin V 5E 7
Sheppard Way BN41: Port 5A 10
Shepway, The BN25: Sea 3G 43
Shepway Pde. BN25: Sea 4D 42
(off Broad St.)
Sherbourne Cl. BN3: Hove 5D 10
Sherbourne Lodge BN11: Wor . . .1A 34
Sherbourne Rd. BN3: Hove 6D 10
Sherbourne Way BN3: Hove 5D 10
Sherbrooke Cl. BN13: Durr 4F 19
Sheridan Mans. BN3: Hove 2G 27
Sheridan Rd. BN14: Broad 5E 21
Sheridan Ter. BN3: Hove 2G 27
Shermanbury Ct. BN15: Somp . . .5A 22
Shermanbury Rd. BN14: Wor 6B 20
Sherrington Rd. BN2: W'dean . . .2H 31
Sherwood Ri. BN25: Sea 3E 43
Sherwood Rd. BN25: Sea 3E 43
Shetland Ct. BN13: Durr 5D 18
Shield Ter. BN9: New 5F 41
Shingle Rd. BN43: Shor B 4C 24
Shipley Rd. BN2: W'dean 3G 31
Ship St. BN1: Brig 6B 44 (6D 28)
BN9: New 3E 41
BN43: Shor S 3A 24
Ship St. Ct. BN1: Brig 5C 44
Ship St. Gdns.
BN1: Brig 5B 44 (5D 28)
Shirley Av. BN3: Hove 6H 11
Shirley Cl. BN14: Salv 3B 20
BN43: Shor S 2E 25
Shirley Dr. BN3: Hove 5H 11
BN14: Salv 3B 20
Shirley M. BN3: Hove 3H 27
Shirley Rd. BN3: Hove 2A 28
Shirley St. BN3: Hove 3H 27
Shooting Fld. BN44: Stey 2C 4
Shopsdam Rd. BN15: S Lan 6D 22
SHOREHAM
(BRIGHTON CITY) AIRPORT
. . . . .3G 23
SHOREHAM BEACH 4B 24
Shoreham By-Pass
BN15: Shor S 1G 23
BN43: Shor S 1G 23
SHOREHAM-BY-SEA 3B 24
Shoreham-by-Sea Station (Rail)
. . . . .3B 24
Shoreham Ct. BN43: Shor S 2B 24
Shoreham Lighthouse 4F 25
Shoreham Rd. BN44: Up B 5G 5
Short Brow BN25: Sea 3F 43
Shortgate Rd. BN2: Brig 4B 14
Shrewsbury Ct. BN11: Wor 3B 34
Sidehill Dr. BN41: Port 6H 9
Sillwood Ct. BN1: Brig 5C 28
(off Montpelier Rd.)
Sillwood Hall BN1: Brig 5C 28
(off Montpelier Rd.)
Sillwood Pl. BN1: Brig 5C 28
Sillwood Rd. BN1: Brig 5C 28
Sillwood St. BN1: Brig 5C 28
Sillwood Ter. BN1: Brig 5C 28
Silver Birch Dr. BN13: Durr 5D 18
Silver Birches BN1: Brig 1C 28
Silverdale BN11: Wor 1H 35
Silverdale Av. BN3: Hove 3B 28
Silverdale Ct. BN3: Hove 3B 28
Silverdale Dr. BN15: Somp 5A 22
Silverdale Rd. BN3: Hove 3B 28
Sinclair Wlk. BN1: Brig 1C 44
Singleton Cl. BN12: Fer 1B 32
Singleton Cres.
BN12: Fer, Gor S 1B 32
BN12: Gor S 2B 32
Singleton Rd. BN1: Brig 2E 13
Sir George's Pl. BN44: Stey 2B 4
Skyline Vw. BN10: Peace 3H 39
Slindon Av. BN10: Peace 6H 39
(not continuous)
Slindon Cl. BN14: Broad 4D 20
Slindon Rd. BN14: Broad 4D 20
Slinfold Cl. BN2: Brig 5H 29
Sloane Ct. BN2: Brig 5G 29
(off Park St.)
SLONK HILL 1D 24
Slonk Hill Rd. BN43: Shor S 6B 8
(not continuous)
Smugglers La. BN44: Up B 4G 5
Smugglers Wlk. BN12: Gor S . . .3G 33
Solway Av. BN1: Brig 1D 12
Somerhill Av. BN3: Hove 3B 28
Somerhill Ct. BN3: Hove 3B 28
(off Somerhill Av.)
Somerhill Lodge BN3: Hove 4B 28
(off Somerhill Rd.)
Somerhill Rd. BN3: Hove 4B 28
Somerset Cl. BN13: W Tar 5A 20
Somerset Cotts. BN13: Clap 1B 18
(off The Street)
Somerset Ct. BN3: Hove 3A 28
(off Wilbury Vs.)
Somerset Point BN2: Brig 6G 29
(off Somerset St.)
Somerset Rd. BN12: Fer 4B 32
Somerset St. BN2: Brig 5G 29
SOMPTING 4H 21
Sompting Av. BN14: Broad 5D 20
Sompting By-Pass
BN14: Char D, Somp 3E 21
Sompting Cl. BN2: Brig 3B 30
Sompting Ct. BN43: Shor S 2D 24
Sompting Rd. BN14: Broad 3E 21
BN15: Lan 4B 22
Sonnet Ct. BN11: Wor 2C 34
(off Shelley Rd.)
Sopers La. BN44: Bramb 6A 4
Sorlings Reach BN43: Shor B . . .4D 24
Southall Av. BN2: Brig 6H 13
Southampton St. BN2: Brig 4F 29
South Ash BN44: Stey 2C 4
South Av. BN2: Brig 5G 29
BN12: Gor S 3G 33
South Bank Ct. BN15: S Lan 6E 23
South Beach BN43: Shor B 4B 24
South Cliffe BN7: Lew 4G 17
Sth. Coast Rd. BN2: Salt 4B 38
BN10: Peace, Salt, Tel C 4B 38
South Ct. BN7: Lew 4G 17
(off Cliffe High St.)
Southcourt Rd. BN14: Broad 1C 34
Southdown Av. BN1: Brig 1E 29
BN7: Lew 5C 16
BN10: Peace 6H 39
(not continuous)
BN41: Port 2C 26
Southdown Cvn. Pk.
BN5: S Dole 4H 5
Southdown Cl. BN9: New 5D 40
Southdown Cnr. BN25: Sea 5F 43
(off Chyngton Rd.)
Southdown Ho. BN3: Hove 3B 28
(off Somerhill Av.)
BN12: Gor S 2F 33
(off Goring Rd.)
Southdown M. BN2: Brig 5G 29
Southdown Pl. BN1: Brig 1E 29
BN7: Lew 3G 17
Southdown Rd. BN1: Brig 6E 13
BN9: New 5D 40
BN25: Sea 4E 43
BN41: Port 6A 10
BN42: S'wick 3G 25
BN43: Shor S 2A 24
Sth. Downs Bus. Pk.
BN7: Lew 3G 17
South Downs National Pk. 3D 8
Southdown Sports Club 6E 17
Sth. Downs Rd. BN7: Lew 3F 17
Southdown Ter. BN44: Stey 3D 4
(off Station Rd.)
Southdownview Cl.
BN14: Broad 5E 21
Southdownview Rd.
BN14: Broad 4E 21
Southdownview Way
BN14: Broad 4E 21
South Dr. BN12: Fer 4A 32
Southease BN2: Brig 5B 30
(off Whitehawk Rd.)
SOUTHERHAM 6H 17
Southerham Rdbt. BN8: Lew 6H 17
SOUTHERN CROSS 1A 26
Southern Ring Rd. BN1: Falm . . .2D 14
Southey Rd. BN11: Wor 3C 34
Sth. Farm Industries
BN14: Wor 5C 20
Sth. Farm Rd. BN11: Wor 4C 20
BN14: Broad 4C 20
Southfield Rd. BN14: Broad 5D 20
SOUTH HEIGHTON 1G 41
SOUTH LANCING 5E 23
Southlands Ct. BN43: Shor S . . .2C 24
SOUTHLANDS HOSPITAL 2D 24
South La. BN9: New 4F 41
(off High St.)
South Lodge BN2: Brig 5B 30
BN15: Somp 3A 22
(off Cokeham Rd.)
SOUTH MALLING 3F 17
Southmount BN1: Brig 1F 29
Southon Cl. BN41: Port 5H 9
Southon Vw. BN15: Lan 6A 22
(off Western Rd.)
SOUTHOVER 5E 17
Southover Grange Gdns. 5E 17
Southover High St. BN7: Lew . . .5D 16
Southover Mnr. Ho. BN7: Lew . . .5E 17
(off Southover High St.)
Southover Pl. BN2: Brig 3F 29
Southover Rd. BN7: Lew 5E 17
Southover St. BN2: Brig 3F 29
South Pl. BN7: Lew 4F 17
(off St John St.)
South Point BN43: Shor B 4C 24
South Rd. BN1: Brig 1C 28
BN9: New 4F 41
South Rd. M. BN1: Brig 1C 28
Southsea Av. BN12: Gor S 2G 33
South St. BN1: Brig 5B 44 (5D 28)
BN1: Falm 2E 15
BN7: Lew 4G 17
(not continuous)
BN8: Lew 4G 17
BN11: Wor 2D 34
BN14: W Tar 6A 20
BN15: Lan 6C 22
BN25: Sea 5D 42
BN41: Port 1A 26
Southview Cl. BN42: S'wick 1G 25
BN43: Shor S 3E 25
Southview Dr. BN11: Wor 2A 34
Southview Gdns. BN11: Wor 2A 34
Southview Rd. BN10: Peace 4G 39
BN14: Fin 2C 6
BN42: S'wick 2G 25
South Vw. Ter. BN9: S Heig 1F 41
Southwater Cl. BN2: Brig 4H 29
BN12: Gor S 1D 32
South Way BN7: Lew 4C 16
BN9: New 4E 41
BN25: Sea 5G 43
Southways Av. BN14: Broad 4E 21
SOUTHWICK 3G 25
Southwick Leisure Cen. 3H 25
Southwick Sq. BN42: S'wick 3G 25
Southwick Station (Rail) 3G 25
Southwick St. BN42: S'wick 3G 25
Southwick Tunnel BN42: S'wick . . .5F 9
BN43: Shor S 5F 9
Southwold Cl. BN13: High S 1G 19
South Woodlands BN1: Brig 3C 12
Sovereign Cl. BN25: Sea 2F 43
Sovereign Ct. BN2: Brig 1A 36
Spa Ct. BN3: Hove 5H 27
(off King's Esplanade)
Sparrows, The BN10: Peace 3H 39
Spears Wlk. BN2: W'dean 2F 31
Speedwell Cl. BN13: Durr 5C 18
Spencer Av. BN3: Hove 5D 10
Spencer Rd. BN15: Lan 5B 22
Spences Ct. BN7: Lew 3G 17
Spences Fld. BN7: Lew 2G 17
Spences La. BN7: Lew 3F 17
Spey Cl. BN13: Durr 2E 19
Spinnals Gro. BN42: S'wick 3F 25
Spinney, The BN3: Hove 5A 12
Spinneys, The BN7: Lew 3G 17
Spital Rd. BN7: Lew 4C 16
Sportcentre Rd. BN1: Falm 2C 14
Springate Rd. BN42: S'wick 2H 25
Springfield Av. BN10: Tel C 4D 38
Springfield Gdns. BN13: Salv . . .3A 20
Springfield Rd. BN1: Brig 2D 28
Spring Gdns.
BN1: Brig 4B 44 (5E 29)
BN7: Lew 4F 17
BN42: S'wick 3G 25
Spring St. BN1: Brig 4A 44 (5C 28)
Squadron Dr. BN13: Durr 4D 18
Square, The BN1: Brig 2C 12
BN14: Fin 2C 6
Stable La. BN14: Fin 2C 6
Stafford Ct. BN25: Sea 4D 42
(off Stafford Rd.)
Stafford Rd. BN1: Brig 2C 28
BN25: Sea 4D 42
Stamford Lodge BN1: Brig 6C 12
(off Cumberland Rd.)
Standean Cl. BN1: Brig 2H 13
Standen Ct. BN44: Up B 5G 5
(off Downscroft)
Stanford Av. BN1: Brig 2D 28
Stanford Cl. BN3: Hove 1A 28
Stanford Ct. BN1: Brig 2D 28
(off Stanford Av.)
Stanford Rd. BN1: Brig 2C 28
Stanford Sq. BN11: Wor 2E 35
Stanhope Rd. BN11: Wor 1D 34
Stanley Av. BN41: Port 4H 9
Stanley Av. Sth. BN41: Port 5H 9
Stanley Deason Leisure Cen. . . .5B 30
Stanley Rd. BN1: Brig 3E 29
BN10: Peace 3F 39
BN11: Wor 1D 34
BN41: Port 2A 26
Stanley St. BN2: Brig 5F 29
STANMER 1B 14
Stanmer Av. BN2: Salt 1B 38
Stanmer Ct. BN1: Brig 6E 13
(off Stanmer Pk. Rd.)
BN1: Falm 2C 14

Stanmer Heights—Tilsmore

STANMER HEIGHTS 2F 13
Stanmer Ho. *BN1: Brig* *6E 13*
(off Stanmer Pk. Rd.)
Stanmer House (Mus.) **1B 14**
Stanmer Pk. Rd. BN1: Brig 6E **13**
Stanmer St. BN1: Brig 6F **13**
Stanmer Vs. BN1: Brig 5F **13**
Stansfield Rd. BN7: Lew 3D **16**
Stanstead Cres. BN2: W'dean . . .4H **31**
Staplefield Dr. BN2: Brig 5B **14**
Stapley Ct. BN3: Hove 2D **26**
Stapley Rd. BN3: Hove 2D **26**
Starboard Ct. BN2: Brig 5B **36**
Star Gallery, The *4E 17*
(off Fisher St.)
Station App. BN1: Falm 2D **14**
BN3: Hove 2H **27**
BN25: Sea 4D **42**
BN43: Shor S *3B 24*
(off Brunswick Rd.)
Station Pde. BN11: Wor 1A **34**
BN15: Lan 5C **22**
Station Rd. BN1: Brig 5B **12**
BN7: Lew 5F **17**
BN9: New 2H **41**
BN11: Wor 1D **34**
BN25: Sea 3A **42**
BN41: Port 4C **26**
BN42: S'wick 3G **25**
BN44: Stey 3D **4**
Station St. BN1: Brig 2C **44** (4E **29**)
BN7: Lew 4F **17**
Steep Cl. BN14: Fin 3C **6**
Steepdown Rd. BN15: Somp 2A **22**
Steep La. BN14: Fin 3C **6**
Steeple Vw. BN13: W Tar 5A **20**
Steine Gdns. **6D 44**
Steine Gdns.
BN2: Brig 5D **44** (5E **29**)
Steine La. BN1: Brig 5C **44**
Steine St. BN2: Brig 6D **44** (6E **29**)
Stephens Rd. BN1: Brig 6F **13**
Stepney Ct. BN1: Brig 1C **44**
Stevens Ct. BN3: Hove 3E **27**
Stevenson Rd. BN2: Brig 5G **29**
Stewards Inn La. BN7: Lew 5E **17**
Steyne, The BN11: Wor 2E **35**
BN25: Sea 5D **42**
Steyne Cl. BN25: Sea 5E **43**
Steyne Ct. BN25: Sea 5D **42**
Steyne Gdns. BN11: Wor 2E **35**
Steyne Rd. BN25: Sea 5D **42**
STEYNING 3C **4**
Steyning Av. BN3: Hove 5F **11**
BN10: Peace 6G **39**
(not continuous)
Steyning By-Pass
BN44: Bramb, Up B 4D **4**
BN44: Stey 1B **4**
Steyning Cl. BN12: Gor S 1E **33**
BN15: Somp 2B **22**
BN25: Sea 5H **43**
Steyning Ct. BN3: Hove 3H **27**
Steyning Ho. BN14: Broad 5D **20**
Steyning Leisure Cen. **2B 4**
Steyning Mus. **3C 4**
Steyning Rd. BN2: Rott 3F **37**
BN25: Sea 5H **43**
Stirling Av. BN25: Sea 3H **43**
Stirling Cl. BN25: Sea 4H **43**
Stirling Ct. BN3: Hove 3A **28**
Stirling Pl. BN3: Hove 3G **27**
Stoke Abbott Ct. *BN11: Wor* *2D 34*
(off Stoke Abbott Rd.)
Stoke Abbott Rd. BN11: Wor 2D **34**
Stoke Cl. BN25: Sea 4G **43**
Stoke Mnr. Cl. BN25: Sea 3G **43**
Stone Cl. BN13: Durr 4H **19**
Stonecroft BN44: Stey 3C **4**
Stonecroft Cl. BN3: Hove 4E **11**
Stonecross Rd. BN2: Brig 4B **14**
STONEHAM 1G **17**
Stoneham Cl. BN7: Lew 2E **17**
Stoneham Rd. BN3: Hove 3F **27**
Stonehurst Ct. BN2: Brig 4G **29**
Stonehurst Rd. BN13: W Tar 5H **19**
Stone La. BN13: Salv 4H **19**
Stoneleigh Av. BN1: Brig 2D **12**
Stoneleigh Cl. BN1: Brig 2D **12**
Stonery Cl. BN41: Port 6A **10**
(not continuous)
Stonery Rd. BN41: Port 6A **10**
Stone St. BN1: Brig 4A **44** (5C **28**)
Stonewood Cl. BN25: Sea 3H **43**
Stoney La. BN43: Shor S 3E **25**
Stopham Cl. BN14: Wor 5B **20**
Storrington Cl. BN3: Hove 6E **11**
Storrington Ri. BN14: Fin V 4D **6**
Stour Cl. BN13: Durr 2E **19**
Stour Rd. BN13: Durr 2E **19**
Strand, The BN2: Brig 5B **36**
BN12: Fer 4A **32**
BN12: Gor S 1D **32**
Strand Pde. BN12: Gor S 6F **19**
Strand Pde. Rdbt. *BN12: Wor* . . .*1G 33*
(off The Boulevard)
Stratheden Ct. BN25: Sea 5D **42**
Strathmore Cl. BN13: Wor 6G **19**
Strathmore Rd. BN13: Wor 6G **19**
Street, The BN13: Clap 1A **18**
BN13: Pat 1A **18**
BN15: N Lan 2C **22**
BN43: Shor S 2H **23**
BN44: Bramb 4E **5**
Street Barn BN15: Somp 3G **21**
Stretton Ct. *BN3: Hove* *3F 27*
(off Rutland Gdns.)
Stringer Way BN1: Brig 5D **12**
Strone Ct. BN11: Wor 3H **33**
Stroudley Rd.
BN1: Brig 1B **44** (3D **28**)
Stuart Cl. BN11: Wor 6F **21**
Styles Fld. *BN7: Lew* *4F 17*
(off Friar's Wlk.)
Sudeley Pl. BN2: Brig 6H **29**
Sudeley St. BN2: Brig 6H **29**
Sudeley Ter. BN2: Brig 6H **29**
Suffolk Ho. BN11: Wor 1D **34**
Suffolk St. BN3: Hove 2F **27**
Sugden Rd. BN11: Wor 1F **35**
Sullington Cl. BN2: Brig 4B **14**
Sullington Gdns. BN14: Fin V 4D **6**
Sullington Way BN43: Shor S . . .2C **24**
Summer Cl. BN41: Port 3A **26**
Summerdale Rd. BN3: Hove 6D **10**
Summerdown Cl. BN13: Durr 5D **18**
Summerdown Ct. *BN13: Durr* *5D 18*
(off Summerdown Cl.)
Summerfields BN14: Fin 2C **6**
Summersdeane BN42: S'wick 1H **25**
Suncourt BN11: Wor 3A **34**
Sunningdale Cl. BN25: Sea 5F **43**
Sunningdale Ct. BN12: Gor S . . .1E **33**
Sunningdale Rd. BN13: Durr 4F **19**
Sunninghill Av. BN3: Hove 6E **11**
Sunninghill Cl. BN3: Hove 6E **11**
Sunny Cl. BN12: Gor S 3G **33**
Sunnydale Av. BN1: Brig 2E **13**
Sunnydale Cl. BN1: Brig 2E **13**
Sunnyside Pk. BN25: Sea 3A **42**
Sunset Cl. BN10: Tel C 2F **39**
Sun St. BN7: Lew 4E **17**
Sunview Av. BN10: Peace 6H **39**
(not continuous)
Surrendean Ct. *BN1: Brig* *5D 12*
(off Varndean Gdns.)
Surrenden Cl. BN1: Brig 4D **12**
Surrenden Cres. BN1: Brig 5C **12**
Surrenden Holt BN1: Brig 5D **12**
Surrenden Lodge BN1: Brig 6D **12**
Surrenden Pk. BN1: Brig 4E **13**
Surrenden Rd. BN1: Brig 5D **12**
Surrey Cl. BN25: Sea 3B **42**
Surrey Ho. BN2: Brig 6H **29**
Surrey Rd. BN25: Sea 3B **42**
Surrey St. BN1: Brig 2B **44** (4D **28**)
BN11: Wor 3C **34**
Surry Ct. *BN43: Shor S* *3B 24*
(off Surry St.)
Surry St. BN43: Shor S 3B **24**
SUSSEX BEACON (HOSPICE), THE
. . . .**1A 30**
Sussex County Cricket Ground
. . . .**3A 28**
Sussex County Lawn Tennis & Croquet Club *3F 25*
(off Victoria Rd.)
Sussex Ct. BN3: Hove 4A **28**
BN43: Shor B 4C **24**
SUSSEX EYE HOSPITAL **6H 29**
Sussex Hgts. BN1: Brig 5A **44**
Sussex Ho. BN10: Tel C 5D **38**
Sussex Ho. Bus. Pk.
BN3: Hove 2F **27**
Sussex M. BN2: Brig 4A **36**
Sussex Pl. BN2: Brig 4F **29**
Sussex Rd. BN3: Hove 5H **27**
BN11: Wor 1D **34**
BN15: S Lan 5G **23**
Sussex Sq. BN2: Brig 4A **36**
Sussex Sq. M. *BN2: Brig* *4A 36*
(off Bristol Pl.)
Sussex St. BN2: Brig 4F **29**
Sussex Ter. BN2: Brig 4F **29**
Sussex Toy & Model Mus.
. . . . **2C 44 (4E 29)**
Sussex University Sports Cen.
. . . . **2C 14**
Sussex Way BN10: Tel C 5D **38**
Sussex Wharf BN43: Shor B 4D **24**
Sussex Yacht Club **4H 25**
Sutherland Rd. BN2: Brig 5G **29**
SUTTON 3G **43**
Sutton Av. BN10: Peace 5F **39**
BN25: Sea 5F **43**
Sutton Av. Nth. BN10: Peace 4F **39**
Sutton Cl. BN2: W'dean 1G **31**
Sutton Ct. BN14: Fin V 5D **6**
Sutton Cft. La. BN25: Sea 4D **42**
Sutton Drove BN25: Sea 3E **43**
Sutton Pk. Rd. BN25: Sea 4D **42**
Sutton Pl. BN25: Sea 3G **43**
Sutton Rd. BN25: Sea 4D **42**
Swallow Ct. *BN2: Brig* *3B 30*
(off Albourne Cl.)
Swallowmead BN44: Stey 4C **4**
Swallows, The BN10: Tel C 3F **39**
Swallows Cl. BN15: S Lan 5G **23**
Swallows Grn. Dr. BN13: Durr . . .5E **19**
Swanborough Ct.
BN43: Shor S *3B 24*
(off New Rd.)
Swanborough Dr. BN2: Brig 3B **30**
Swanborough Pl. BN2: Brig 3B **30**
Swanbourne Cl. BN15: N Lan . . .2D **22**
Swandean Cl. BN13: High S 2G **19**
Swannee Cl. BN10: Peace 3H **39**
Sweda Ct. BN2: Brig 6H **29**
Swing Bri. BN9: New 3F **41**
Swiss Gdns. BN43: Shor S 3A **24**
Sycamore Cl. BN2: W'dean 2G **31**
BN13: Durr 4E **19**
BN25: Sea 4H **43**
BN41: Port 5C **10**
(not continuous)
Sycamore Ct. *BN2: Brig* *2H 29*
(off Fitzherbert Dr.)
Sycamores, The BN10: Peace . . .3G **39**
Sydney St. BN1: Brig 3C **44** (4E **29**)
Sydney Tidy Ho. *BN2: Brig* *4G 29*
(off Queen's Pk. Rd.)
Sylvan Rd. BN15: Somp 4H **21**
Sylvester Way BN3: Hove 5C **10**
Symbister Rd. BN41: Port 3C **26**

T

Talbot Cres. BN1: Brig 2H **13**
Talbot Ter. BN7: Lew 4E **17**
Talland Pde. BN25: Sea 5D **42**
Tamar Av. BN13: Durr 2E **19**
Tamar Cl. BN13: Durr 3E **19**
Tamarisk Way BN12: Fer 3B **32**
Tamplin Ter. BN2: Brig 4F **29**
Tamworth Rd. BN3: Hove 3F **27**
Tandridge Rd. BN3: Hove 4E **27**
Tangmere Pl. BN1: Brig 2E **13**
Tangmere Rd. BN1: Brig 2E **13**
Tanners Brook BN7: Lew 5F **17**
Tanyard Cotts. BN44: Stey 3B **4**
Tanyard La. BN44: Stey 3B **4**
Tarmount La. BN43: Shor S 3B **24**
Tarner Rd. BN2: Brig 4F **29**
Tarragon Way BN43: Shor S 1E **25**
Tarring Cl. BN9: S Heig 1F **41**
Tarring Ga. BN14: W Tar 6A **20**
Tarring Rd. BN11: Wor 1H **33**
Tasman Way BN13: Durr 3E **19**
Taunton Gro. BN2: Brig 1C **30**
Taunton Pl. *BN2: Brig* *1C 30*
(off Taunton Rd.)
Taunton Rd. BN2: Brig 1B **30**
Taunton Way BN2: Brig 1C **30**
Tavern Pl. BN1: Brig 5E **29**
Tavistock Down BN1: Brig 6G **13**
Tavy Cl. BN13: Durr 4E **19**
Tavy Rd. BN13: Durr 4E **19**
Taw Cl. BN13: Durr 3F **19**
Teg Cl. BN41: Port 6B **10**
Teign Wlk. *BN13: Durr* *2E 19*
(off Adur Av.)
Telegraph St. BN2: Brig 6G **29**
Telgarth Rd. BN12: Fer 4A **32**
TELSCOMBE 1F **39**
TELSCOMBE CLIFFS 5E **39**
Telscombe Cliffs Way
BN10: Tel C 5D **38**
Telscombe Cl. BN10: Peace 2H **39**
Telscombe Grange
BN10: Tel C 5D **38**
Telscombe Pk. BN10: Peace 2G **39**
Telscombe Rd.
BN10: Peace, Tel C 2E **39**
Templars, The BN14: Broad 3E **21**
Temple Gdns. BN1: Brig 4C **28**
Temple Hgts. *BN1: Brig* *4C 28*
(off Windlesham Rd.)
Temple St. BN1: Brig 4C **28**
Ten Acres BN11: Wor 1G **35**
Tenantry Down Rd. BN2: Brig . . .3A **30**
Tenantry Rd. BN2: Brig 2H **29**
Tennis Rd. BN3: Hove 4E **27**
Tennyson Ct. BN3: Hove 3G **27**
Tennyson Rd. BN11: Wor 2C **34**
Terminus Bldgs. *BN25: Sea* *4D 42*
(off Blatchington Rd.)
Terminus Pl.
BN1: Brig 1B **44** (3D **28**)
Terminus Rd.
BN1: Brig 1B **44** (3D **28**)
Terminus St.
BN1: Brig 2B **44** (4D **28**)
Terrace, The BN12: Gor S 2E **33**
BN15: S Lan 6C **22**
Terrace Row *BN2: Brig* *6F 29*
(off Broad St.)
Terringes Av. BN13: Wor 6G **19**
Test Rd. BN15: Somp 4H **21**
Teville Ga. BN11: Wor 1D **34**
Teville Industrials
BN14: Broad 5F **21**
Teville Pl. BN11: Wor 1C **34**
Teville Rd. BN11: Wor 1C **34**
Teynham Ho. BN2: Salt 4A **38**
Thackeray Rd. BN14: Broad 6F **21**
Thakeham Cl. BN12: Gor S 2C **32**
Thakeham Dr. BN12: Gor S 2C **32**
Thalassa Rd. BN11: Wor 1H **35**
Thames Cl. BN2: Brig 5F **29**
Thames Ho. *BN2: Brig* *5F 29*
(off Thames Cl.)
Thames Way BN13: Durr 3F **19**
Thatch Ct. BN15: N Lan 2C **22**
The . . . .
Names prefixed with 'The' for example 'The Acre Cl.' are indexed under the main name such as 'Acre Cl., The'
Theatre Royal . . . . **4C 44 (5E 29)**
Thebes Gallery *4F 17*
(off Church Twitten)
Theobald Ho. BN1: Brig 2C **44**
Thesiger Cl. BN11: Wor 6G **21**
Thesiger Rd. BN11: Wor 6G **21**
Third Av. BN3: Hove 5H **27**
BN9: New 5E **41**
BN14: Char D 3D **20**
BN15: Lan 3C **22**
Third Rd. BN10: Peace 5E **39**
Thirlmere Cres. BN15: Somp 5H **21**
Thomas St. BN7: Lew 3G **17**
Thompson Rd. BN1: Brig 1G **29**
BN9: New 1H **41**
Thomson Cl. BN13: Durr 4D **18**
Thornbush Cres. BN41: Port 5B **10**
Thorndean Rd. BN2: Brig 5H **13**
Thornhill Av. BN1: Brig 1E **13**
Thornhill Cl. BN3: Hove 5E **11**
Thornhill Ri. BN41: Port 4H **9**
Thornhill Way BN41: Port 5A **10**
Thorn Rd. BN11: Wor 3C **34**
Thornscroft BN44: Stey 2C **4**
Thornsdale *BN2: Brig* *4F 29*
(off Albion Hill)
Thurlow Rd. BN11: Wor 1E **35**
Thyme Cl. BN43: Shor S 1E **25**
Ticehurst Rd. BN2: Brig 5B **30**
Tichborne St.
BN1: Brig 4C **44** (5E **29**)
TIDE MILLS 6H **41**
Tide Mills Way BN25: Sea 3A **42**
Tidy St. BN1: Brig 3C **44** (4E **29**)
Tilbury Pl. BN2: Brig 5F **29**
Tilbury Way BN2: Brig 4F **29**
Tilgate Cl. BN2: Brig 4H **29**
Tillington BN2: Brig 3A **30**
Tillstone Cl. BN2: Brig 6H **13**
Tillstone St. BN2: Brig 5F **29**
Tilsmore BN2: Brig 5B **30**

Timber Cl.—Walmer Rd.

Timber Cl. BN13: Durr 4E 19
Timberlane Trad. Est.
BN14: Broad 5F 21
Timber Yd. Cotts. BN7: Lew 4G 17
Timber Yd. La. BN7: Lew 4G 17
Tintagel Ct. BN3: Hove 2G 27
BN43: Shor S 3B 24
Tintern Cl. BN1: Brig 1F 29
Tisbury Rd. BN3: Hove 4H 27
Titch Hill BN15: Somp 1G 21
Tithe Barn BN15: N Lan 2C 22
Titian Rd. BN3: Hove 3F 27
Titnore La. BN12: Gor S 3A 18
BN13: Clap, Gor S, Pat 3A 18
Titnore Way BN13: Durr 4C 18
Tivoli BN1: Brig 6C 12
Tivoli Cres. BN1: Brig 1B 28
Tivoli Cres. Nth. BN1: Brig 6B 12
Tivoli Pl. BN1: Brig 6B 12
Tivoli Rd. BN1: Brig 6B 12
Tollbridge Ho. BN43: Shor S 2H 23
Tollgate BN10: Peace 3F 39
TONGDEAN 5A 12
Tongdean Av. BN3: Hove 5A 12
Tongdean Ct. BN1: Brig 4B 12
Tongdean La. BN1: Brig 4H 11
(Gableson Av.)
BN1: Brig 4B 12
(Windsor Ct.)
Tongdean Pl. BN3: Hove 5A 12
Tongdean Ri. BN1: Brig 4A 12
Tongdean Rd. BN3: Hove 5H 11
Toomey Rd. BN44: Stey 1C 4
Tophill Cl. BN41: Port 6H 9
Torcross Cl. BN2: Brig 1A 30
Toronto Cl. BN13: Durr 4F 19
Toronto Ter. BN2: Brig 4F 29
BN7: Lew 4E 17
Torrance Cl. BN3: Hove 1F 27
Torridge Cl. BN13: Durr 3E 19
Tor Rd. BN10: Peace 2G 39
Tor Rd. W. BN10: Peace 2G 39
Totland Rd. BN2: Brig 3H 29
Tottington Way BN43: Shor S . . .1D 24
Tourist Info. Cen.
Brighton 5C 44 (5E 29)
Hove 4H 27
Lewes 4F 17
Peacehaven 5G 39
Seaford *4D 42*
(off Clinton Pl.)
Worthing, Chapel Pde. . . .2D 34
Worthing, Marine Pde. . . .3E 35
Tower Ga. BN1: Brig 6C 12
Tower Ho. BN1: Brig 6C 12
Tower Rd. BN2: Brig 4G 29
BN11: Wor 1E 35
BN15: Somp 5A 22
Tower Rd. Flats BN15: Lan 5B 22
Towers Rd. BN44: Up B 4G 5
Tozer Ct. BN41: Port 3B 26
Trafalgar Cl. BN10: Peace 3G 39
Trafalgar Ct.
BN1: Brig 2D 44 (4E 29)
Trafalgar Ga. BN2: Brig 5B 36
Trafalgar La.
BN1: Brig 3C 44 (4E 29)
Trafalgar M. BN1: Brig 2C 44
Trafalgar Pl.
BN1: Brig 2C 44 (4E 29)
Trafalgar Rd. BN41: Port 2B 26
Trafalgar St.
BN1: Brig 2C 44 (4E 29)
Trafalgar Ter. BN1: Brig 3C 44
Trafalgar Vw. BN1: Brig 2C 44
Transit Rd. BN9: New 4F 41
Traslyn Ct. BN11: Wor 2F 35
Tredcroft Rd. BN3: Hove 6H 11
Treetops Cl. BN2: W'dean 2G 31
Treharne Cl. BN13: Durr 3F 19
Tremola Av. BN2: Salt 2H 37
Trent Cl. BN15: Somp 4A 22
Trent Lodge *BN2: Brig* *5F 29*
(off Mt. Pleasant)
Trent Rd. BN12: Gor S 2G 33
Treveor Cl. BN11: Wor 2C 34
Treyford Cl. BN2: W'dean 1G 31
Triangle, The BN15: Lan 6A 22
BN43: Shor S 2B 24
Trinity St. BN2: Brig 3F 29
Tristram Cl. BN15: Somp 3H 21
Troon Cl. BN25: Sea 1A 42
Truleigh Cl. BN2: W'dean 3H 31
Truleigh Ct. *BN44: Up B* *4G 5*
(off Truleigh Rd.)
Truleigh Dr. BN41: Port 4A 10
Truleigh Rd. BN44: Up B 4G 5
Truleigh Way BN43: Shor S 1C 24
Truro Ct. *BN11: Wor* *3A 34*
(off Pevensey Gdns.)
Tudor Cl. BN2: Rott 2G 37
BN3: Hove 6F 11
BN14: Fin 2C 6
BN15: S Lan 4F 23
BN25: Sea 3C 42
Tudor Dr. BN44: Up B 3F 5
Tudor Rose Pk. BN10: Peace 5B 40
Tudors, The *BN3: Hove* *1F 27*
(off Wayfield Av.)
Tumulus Rd. BN2: Salt 2A 38
Tunsgate BN44: Stey 3C 4
Turner Ho. *BN41: Port* *3C 26*
(off Gordon Cl.)
Turner Rd. BN14: Broad 4E 21
Turnpike Cl. BN10: Peace 3G 39
Turnpike Piece BN1: Falm 2D 14
Turton Cl. BN2: Brig 5H 29
Tuscan Ct. BN10: Tel C 5D 38
Twineham Cl. BN2: Brig 3B 30
Twitten, The BN2: Rott 3G 37
BN42: S'wick 3G 25
BN44: Up B 5G 5
Twitten Cl. BN42: S'wick 3G 25
Twittenside BN44: Stey 4C 4
Twitten Way BN14: Wor 6A 20
Twyford Cl. BN13: Durr 4G 19
Twyford Gdns. BN13: Durr 4G 19
Twyford Rd. BN1: Brig 2A 14
BN13: Durr 4G 19
Tye Cl. BN2: Salt 4B 38
Tyedean Rd. BN10: Tel C 4D 38
Tye Vw. BN10: Tel C 3E 39
Tyne Cl. BN13: Durr 3E 19
Tynings, The BN15: Lan 5B 22
Tyson Pl. *BN2: Brig* *5F 29*
(off Grosvenor St.)

U

Uckfield Cl. BN2: Brig 4B 30
Ullswater Rd. BN15: Somp 5H 21
Undercliff Wlk.
BN2: Brig, O'dean, Rott 1B 36
Underdown Rd. BN42: S'wick . . .2G 25
Undermill Rd. BN44: Up B 4G 5
Union Pl. BN11: Wor 2D 34
Union Rd. BN2: Brig 3F 29
Union St. BN1: Brig 5C 44
University of Brighton
Circus St. Annexe 4D 44
Falmer Campus 3D 14
Grand Pde. 4D 44
Mithras House 1G 29
Moulsecoomb Campus . . .6G 13
University of Brighton Annexe
. . . . .5D 44
University of Sussex 1D 14
Uplands Av. BN13: High S 1H 19
Uplands Rd. BN1: Brig 6G 13
Up. Abbey Rd. BN2: Brig 6H 29
Up. Bannings Rd. BN2: Salt 1C 38
Up. Bedford St. BN2: Brig 6G 29
UPPER BEEDING 4F 5
Upper Beeding Sports & Youth Cen.
. . . . .4F 5
Up. Belgrave Rd. BN25: Sea 3D 42
UPPER BEVENDEAN 1E 31
Up. Bevendean Av. BN2: Brig . . .1A 30
Up. Boundstone La.
BN15: Lan, Somp 3B 22
(not continuous)
Up. Brighton Rd.
BN14: Broad, Char D 4C 20
BN15: N Lan, Somp 3F 21
Up. Chalvington Pl.
BN2: Brig 5A 30
Up. Chyngton Gdns.
BN25: Sea 3G 43
UPPER COKEHAM 3A 22
Upper Cotts. BN2: O'dean 6F 31
Upper Dr., The BN3: Hove 2A 28
Up. Gardner St.
BN1: Brig 3C 44 (4E 29)
Up. Gloucester Rd.
BN1: Brig 2B 44 (4D 28)
Up. Hamilton Rd. BN1: Brig 2C 28
Up. High St. BN11: Wor 1E 35
Up. Hollingdean Rd.
BN1: Brig 1F 29
Up. Kingston La.
BN42: S'wick 1F 25
BN43: Shor S 1F 25
Up. Lewes Rd. BN2: Brig 3F 29
Upper Mkt. St. BN3: Hove 5B 28
Upper Nth. St.
BN1: Brig 3A 44 (4C 28)
Up. Park Pl. BN2: Brig 5F 29
Up. Rock Gdns. BN2: Brig 5F 29
Up. Roedale Cotts.
BN1: Brig 4E 13
Up. St James's St. BN2: Brig 6F 29
Up. Sherwood Rd. BN25: Sea . . .3E 43
Up. Shoreham Rd.
BN43: Shor S 2H 23
Upper Stoneham BN8: Lew 1H 17
Up. Sudeley St. BN2: Brig 6H 29
Up. Valley Rd. BN9: New 5D 40
Up. Wellington Rd. BN2: Brig . . .3G 29
Up. West Dr. BN12: Fer 3A 32
Up. West La. BN15: N Lan 2C 22
Up. Winfield Av. BN1: Brig 2D 12
Upton Av. BN42: S'wick 1G 25
Upton Ct. BN13: Wor 1H 33
Upton Gdns. BN13: Wor 6H 19
Upton Rd. BN13: Wor 6H 19

V

VALE, THE 4C 6
Vale, The BN2: O'dean 5G 31
Vale Av. BN1: Brig 1C 12
BN14: Fin V 6D 6
Vale Cl. BN25: Sea 3F 43
Vale Ct. BN41: Port 3B 26
Vale Dr. BN14: Fin V 6D 6
Vale Gdns. BN41: Port 3B 26
Valence Rd. BN7: Lew 4D 16
Valencia Rd. BN11: Wor 1A 34
Valentine Cl. BN14: Salv 3B 20
BN43: Shor S *1H 23*
(off Steyning Rd.)
Valentine Ct. BN3: Hove 3A 28
Valerie Cl. BN41: Port 6B 10
Vale Rd. BN2: Salt 1B 38
BN25: Sea 3E 43
BN41: Port 3B 26
Vale Wlk. BN14: Fin V 1H 19
Vallance Ct. *BN3: Hove* *4G 27*
(off Hove St.)
Vallance Gdns. BN3: Hove 4G 27
Vallance Rd. BN3: Hove 4G 27
Vallensdean Cotts.
BN41: Port 6C 10
Valley Cl. BN1: Brig 4A 12
BN9: New 3D 40
Valley Dene BN9: New 4D 40
Valley Dr. BN1: Brig 4H 11
BN25: Sea 2F 43
Valley Fld. Ct. BN14: Fin V 5D 6
Valley Gdns. BN14: Fin V 1A 20
Valley Ri. BN25: Sea 3E 43
Valley Rd. BN7: Lew 5C 16
BN9: New 4D 40
BN10: Peace 2G 39
BN15: Somp 2A 22
BN41: Port 5H 9
Valverde Ho. BN3: Hove 3A 28
Vanburgh Ct. BN3: Hove 3H 27
Vancouver Cl. BN13: Durr 4F 19
Vancouver Rd. BN13: Durr 4E 19
Vantage Point *BN1: Brig* *3E 29*
(off New England Rd.)
Varey Rd. BN13: Durr 4D 18
Varndean Cl. BN1: Brig 5C 12
Varndean Dr. BN1: Brig 5C 12
Varndean Gdns. BN1: Brig 5C 12
Varndean Holt BN1: Brig 5D 12
Varndean Rd. BN1: Brig 5C 12
Ventnor Vs. BN3: Hove 4H 27
Vere Rd. BN1: Brig 2E 29
Veric BN3: Hove 3A 28
Vernon Av. BN2: W'dean 1E 31
BN10: Peace 6H 39
(not continuous)
Vernon Ct. *BN1: Brig* *4C 28*
(off Windlesham Av.)
Vernon Gdns. *BN1: Brig* *4C 28*
(off Denmark Ter.)
Vernon Ter.
BN1: Brig 2A 44 (4C 28)
Veronica Way BN2: Brig 6F 29
Verralls Wlk. BN7: Lew 5E 17
Viaduct Rd. BN1: Brig 3E 29
Vicarage Cl. BN9: New 1G 41
BN25: Sea 4E 43
Vicarage Flds. BN13: Durr 3F 19
Vicarage La. BN2: Rott 3F 37
BN44: Stey 3C 4
Vicarage Ter. BN2: Rott 3F 37
Viceroy Ct. BN12: Fer 3A 32
Viceroy Lodge BN3: Hove 4G 27
Victor Cl. BN25: Sea 2C 42
Victoria Av. BN10: Peace 6G 39
(not continuous)
Victoria Cotts. *BN3: Hove* *5H 27*
(off Sussex Rd.)
Victoria Ct. BN3: Hove 4H 27
BN11: Wor 1C 34
(Clifton Gdns.)
BN11: Wor 1C 34
(Victoria Rd.)
BN15: Lan 6C 22
BN41: Port 2C 26
BN43: Shor S *3A 24*
(off Victoria Rd.)
Victoria Gro. BN3: Hove 4A 28
VICTORIA HOSPITAL (LEWES)
. . . . .4C 16
Victoria M. *BN2: Rott* *3F 37*
(off West St.)
Victoria Pk. Gdns. BN11: Wor . . .1C 34
BN41: Port *2C 26*
(off Old Shoreham Rd.)
Victoria Pl.
BN1: Brig 3A 44 (4C 28)
Victoria Rd.
BN1: Brig 3A 44 (4C 28)
BN11: Wor 1C 34
BN41: Port 2B 26
BN42: S'wick 3F 25
BN43: Shor S 3A 24
Victoria Rd. Trad. Est.
BN41: Port 2C 26
Victoria St.
BN1: Brig 3A 44 (4C 28)
Victoria Ter. BN3: Hove 5H 27
Victory M. BN2: Brig 1A 36
View Rd. BN10: Peace 4G 39
Viking Cl. BN25: Sea 1A 42
Village Barn, The BN1: Brig 1C 12
Village Cl. BN41: Port 6B 10
Village Grn. BN9: Pidd 1D 40
Village Sq. BN2: Brig 5B 36
Village Way BN1: Falm 2D 14
Villiers Cl. BN2: W'dean 2G 31
Villiers Ct. BN1: Brig 2C 44
Vincent Cl. BN15: Lan 4B 22
Vincent's Ct. BN2: Brig 1A 36
Vine Pl. BN1: Brig 3A 44 (4D 28)
Vineries, The BN3: Hove 4C 28
Vineries Cl. BN13: Salv 4A 20
Vinery Ct. BN13: Salv 4A 20
Vines Cross Rd. BN2: Brig 3B 30
Vine St. BN1: Brig 3D 44 (4E 29)
Vogue Gyratory BN2: Brig 2G 29
Volk's Electric Railway 6F 29

W

Wadhurst Ct. BN11: Wor 1A 34
Wadhurst Dr. BN12: Gor S 2D 32
Wadhurst Ri. BN2: Brig 5B 30
Wadurs Swimming Pool 1F 25
Waite Cl. BN7: Lew 3F 17
Wakefield Pl. *BN2: Brig* *2F 29*
(off Wakefield Rd.)
Wakefield Rd. BN2: Brig 2F 29
Wakehurst Ct. BN11: Wor 1F 35
Walberton Ct. BN11: Wor 3H 33
Waldegrave Ct. *BN2: Salt* *1B 38*
(off Westfield Av.)
Waldegrave Rd. BN1: Brig 6D 12
Waldron Av. BN1: Brig 2H 13
Waldron Pl. BN1: Brig 2H 13
Waldshut Rd. BN7: Lew 2C 16
Walesbeech Rd. BN2: Salt 4B 38
Wallace Av. BN11: Wor 2H 33
Wallace Ct. BN11: Wor 2H 33
Wallace M. BN11: Wor 3H 33
Wallace Pde. *BN11: Wor* *2H 33*
(off Goring Rd.)
Wallands Cres. BN7: Lew 3E 17
WALLANDS PARK 4D 16
Wallands Pk. Ri. BN7: Lew 4D 16
Walmer Cl. BN2: Brig 1D 30
Walmer Cres. BN2: Brig 1D 30
Walmer Rd. BN25: Sea 3H 43

66 A-Z Brighton & Worthing

Walnut Cl.—Wilmington Cl.

Walnut Cl. BN1: Brig 5C 12
Walnut Ct. *BN13: Salv 4A 20*
(off Offington La.)
Walnut Lodge BN14: Wor 6C 20
Walnut Tree Way
BN13: Durr 5D 18
Walpole Av. BN12: Gor S 2F 33
Walpole Rd. BN2: Brig 5G 29
Walpole Ter. BN2: Brig 5H 29
Walsingham Rd. BN3: Hove 4F 27
Walter May Ho. *BN2: Brig 5B 30*
(off Whitehawk Rd.)
Walton Bank BN1: Brig 3A 14
Walton Cl. BN13: Durr 4H 19
Walton Lodge BN13: Durr 4H 19
Walwers La. BN7: Lew 4F 17
Wanderdown Cl. BN2: O'dean 6G 31
Wanderdown Dr. BN2: O'dean 6G 31
Wanderdown Rd. BN2: O'dean 6F 31
Wanderdown Way
BN2: O'dean 6G 31
Wantley Rd. BN14: Fin V 1A 20
Warbleton Cl. BN2: Brig 5A 30
Warenne Rd. BN3: Hove 5C 10
Warleigh Rd. BN1: Brig 2E 29
Warmdene Av. BN1: Brig 2D 12
Warmdene Cl. BN1: Brig 3D 12
Warmdene Rd. BN1: Brig 2D 12
Warmdene Way BN1: Brig 2D 12
Warner Rd. BN14: Broad 6F 21
Warners Pde. *BN11: Wor 1C 34*
(off Orme Rd.)
Warnes BN11: Wor 2E 35
Warnham Cl. BN12: Gor S 3F 33
Warnham Ct. BN3: Hove 4H 27
Warnham M. BN12: Gor S 2F 33
Warnham Ri. BN1: Brig 3E 13
Warnham Rd. BN12: Gor S 2F 33
Warren, The BN12: Fer 4B 32
Warren Av. BN2: W'dean 1E 31
Warren Cl. BN2: W'dean 2D 30
BN7: Lew 5D 16
BN14: Salv 3B 20
Warren Ct. BN14: Salv 3B 20
BN15: Lan 5B 22
BN42: S'wick 1G 25
Warren Dr. BN7: Lew 5C 16
Warren Farm Pl. BN14: Fin V 2A 20
Warren Gdns. BN14: Salv 3B 20
Warren Lodge BN10: Tel C 3E 39
Warren Ri. BN2: W'dean 2D 30
Warren Rd.
BN2: Brig, W'dean 3A 30
BN14: Salv 2A 20
Warren Way BN2: W'dean 2F 31
BN10: Tel C 3E 39
Warrior Cl. BN41: Port 6B 10
Warwick Ct. *BN3: Hove 3C 28*
(off Davigdor Rd.)
Warwick Gdns. BN11: Wor 2E 35
Warwick La. *BN11: Wor 2E 35*
(off Warwick St.)
Warwick Mt. *BN2: Brig 6G 29*
(off Montague St.)
Warwick Pl. BN11: Wor 2E 35
Warwick Rd. BN11: Wor 2E 35
BN25: Sea 4D 42
Warwick St. BN11: Wor 2D 34
Warwick Wlk. BN43: Shor S 1B 24
Washington Rd.
BN44: Stey, Wis 1A 4
Washington St. BN2: Brig 4F 29
Waterdyke Av. BN42: S'wick 3G 25
Waterford Cl. BN10: Peace 2G 39
Waterfront, The BN2: Brig 5B 36
Watergate La. BN7: Lew 5E 17
WATERHALL 2H 11
Waterhall Rd. BN1: Brig 2H 11
Water La. BN13: Ang 3A 18
Waterloo Pl. BN2: Brig 4F 29
BN7: Lew 4F 17
Waterloo St. BN3: Hove 5B 28
Watersfield Rd. BN14: Wor 5B 20
Watling Cl. BN42: S'wick 3G 25
Watling Ct. *BN42: S'wick 3G 25*
(off Watling Rd.)
Watling Rd. BN42: S'wick 3G 25
Waverley Ct. BN11: Wor 3B 34
BN25: Sea 5E 43
Waverley Cres. BN1: Brig 1G 29
Wavertree Rd. BN12: Gor S 1F 33
Wayfield Av. BN3: Hove 1E 27
Wayfield Cl. BN3: Hove 1F 27
Wayland Av. BN1: Brig 4A 12
Wayland Hgts. BN1: Brig 4A 12
Wayside BN1: Brig 2B 12
BN15: Lan 5A 22
Wayside Av. BN13: Durr 3F 19
Weald Av. BN3: Hove 1F 27
Weald Cl. BN7: Lew 3E 17
Weald Dyke BN43: Shor B 4B 24
Wear Cl. BN13: Durr 3E 19
Wear Rd. BN13: Durr 3E 19
Weavers Ct. *BN43: Shor S 3A 24*
(off Ropetackle)
Welbeck Av. BN3: Hove 4E 27
Welbeck Ct. BN3: Hove 4E 27
BN25: Sea 4D 42
Welbeck Mans. *BN3: Hove 4E 27*
(off Welbeck Av.)
Welesmere Rd. BN2: Rott 1G 37
Welland Cl. BN13: Durr 2F 19
Welland Rd. BN13: Durr 2F 19
Wellend Vs. BN1: Brig 2D 28
Wellesley Av. BN12: Gor S 2F 33
Wellesley Ct. BN11: Wor 3H 33
Well Ho. Pl. BN7: Lew 4E 17
Wellingham La.
BN13: High S 1G 19
Wellington Ct. *BN2: Brig 3F 29*
(off Wellington Rd.)
BN2: Brig 1A 36
(Victory M.)
BN11: Wor 2A 34
Wellingtonia Ct. *BN1: Brig 5C 12*
(off Laine Cl.)
Wellington Pk. BN25: Sea 4F 43
Wellington Rd. BN2: Brig 3F 29
BN9: New 1G 41
BN10: Peace 5A 40
BN41: Port 4B 26
Wellington St. BN2: Brig 3G 29
BN7: Lew 4F 17
Wellsbourne *BN2: Brig 5B 30*
(off Findon Rd.)
Wells Ct. *BN11: Wor 3A 34*
(off Pevensey Gdns.)
Wembley Av. BN15: Lan 4B 22
Wembley Gdns. BN15: Lan 4B 22
Wenban Pas. *BN11: Wor 1D 34*
(off Wenban Rd.)
Wenban Rd. BN11: Wor 1D 34
Wenceling Cotts.
BN15: S Lan 5G 23
Wendale Dr. BN10: Peace 2H 39
Wendover Grange BN3: Hove 4G 27
Went Hill Pk. BN25: Sea 4F 43
Wentworth Cl. BN13: Durr 2H 19
Wentworth Ct. BN11: Wor 2B 34
Wentworth St. BN2: Brig 6F 29
Weppons BN43: Shor S 3B 24
Wessex Ct. BN11: Wor 2C 34
Wessex Wlk. BN43: Shor S 1B 24
West Av. BN11: Wor 2A 34
BN15: S Lan 5E 23
West Beach BN43: Shor B 5H 23
W. Beach Ct. BN25: Sea 3A 42
WEST BLATCHINGTON 6F 11
West Blatchington Windmill 6F 11
Westbourne Av. BN14: Broad 6D 20
Westbourne Gdns. BN3: Hove 4G 27
Westbourne Gro. BN3: Hove 3G 27
Westbourne Pl. BN3: Hove 4G 27
Westbourne St. BN3: Hove 3G 27
Westbourne Vs. BN3: Hove 4F 27
Westbrook BN2: Salt 2A 38
Westbrooke BN11: Wor 2D 34
Westbrooke Ct. *BN11: Wor 2C 34*
(off Crescent Rd.)
Westbrook Way BN42: S'wick 3H 25
West Bldgs. BN11: Wor 3C 34
Westbury Ct. BN11: Wor 2B 34
Westcombe *BN1: Brig 3C 28*
(off Dyke Rd.)
West Ct. *BN43: Shor S 3A 24*
(off West St.)
Westcourt Pl. BN14: Broad 6C 20
Westcourt Rd. BN14: Broad 1C 34
Westdean Av. BN9: New 6C 40
W. Dean Ri. BN25: Sea 3F 43
Westdean Rd. BN14: Wor 5B 20
WESTDENE 3A 12
Westdene Dr. BN1: Brig 3A 12
Westdown Ct. BN11: Wor 1A 34
Westdown Rd. BN25: Sea 3C 42
West Dr. BN2: Brig 5F 29
BN12: Fer 4A 32
West End Way BN15: Lan 6B 22
Westergate Cl. BN12: Fer 2B 32
Westergate Rd. BN2: Brig 4A 14
Westerman Complex
BN3: Hove 2F 27
Western Cl. BN15: Lan 6A 22
Western Concourse BN2: Brig 6B 36
Western Ct. BN9: New 5E 41
Western Esplanade
BN3: Hove 4D 26
Western Lodge *BN15: Somp 3A 22*
(off Cokeham Rd.)
Western Pl. BN11: Wor 3C 34
Western Rd. BN1: Brig 4B 28
BN3: Hove 4A 44 (4A 28)
BN7: Lew 4D 16
BN9: New 5D 40
BN15: Lan, Somp 5H 21
BN43: Shor S 3B 24
Western Rd. Nth.
BN15: Somp 4A 22
Western Row BN11: Wor 3C 34
Western St. BN1: Brig 5B 28
Western Ter. BN1: Brig 5C 28
BN15: Somp 3F 21
Westfield Av. BN2: Salt 1B 38
Westfield Av. Nth. BN2: Salt 1B 38
Westfield Av. Sth. BN2: Salt 1B 38
Westfield Cl. BN1: Brig 4E 13
Westfield Cres. BN1: Brig 3E 13
Westfield Ri. BN2: Salt 1B 38
Westgate St. BN7: Lew 4E 17
Westham BN2: Brig 5B 30
West Hill BN13: High S 6C 6
W. Hill Cl. BN13: High S 6C 6
W. Hill Pl. BN1: Brig 2B 44 (4D 28)
W. Hill Rd.
BN1: Brig 2A 44 (4D 28)
W. Hill St. BN1: Brig 2A 44 (4D 28)
West Jetty BN2: Brig 6B 36
Westlake Cl. BN13: Wor 5H 19
Westlake Gdns. BN13: Wor 5H 19
Westland Av. BN14: Wor 6A 20
Westland Ct. *BN41: Port 3A 26*
(off West Rd.)
Westlands BN12: Fer 3A 32
West La. BN15: Lan 3C 22
West Mans. BN11: Wor 3B 34
Westmead Gdns. BN11: Wor 2H 33
Westmeston Av. BN2: Salt 2H 37
Westminster Ct. BN11: Wor 2F 35
Westmoreland Wlk.
BN43: Shor S 1A 24
Westmorland Ct. BN3: Hove 1A 44
Westmount BN2: Brig 4G 29
Westmount Cl. BN42: S'wick 2F 25
W. Onslow Cl. BN12: Fer 1A 32
West Pde. BN11: Wor 4H 33
West Pk. La. BN12: Gor S 2G 33
West Pier (disused)
Brighton 6C 28
West Point BN43: Shor B 4C 24
West Quay BN2: Brig 6B 36
BN9: New 5F 41
West Rd. BN41: Port 3A 26
West St. BN1: Brig 5B 44 (5D 28)
BN2: Rott 3F 37
BN7: Lew 4F 17
BN11: Wor 3C 34
BN15: Somp 3F 21
BN25: Sea 5D 42
BN41: Port 3C 26
BN43: Shor S 3A 24
WEST TARRING 5A 20
West Tyne BN13: Durr 4F 19
West Vw. BN3: Hove 3A 28
BN25: Sea 5D 42
West Vw. Cl. BN2: W'dean 2F 31
West Vw. Ct. BN25: Sea 5D 42
West Vw. Ter. BN9: New 1F 41
Westview Ter. *BN14: Fin 2C 6*
(off North Vw. Ter.)
West Way BN3: Hove 6D 10
BN13: High S 1F 19
BN15: S Lan 5E 23
Westway Cl. BN41: Port 4G 9
Westway Gdns. BN41: Port 4G 9
WEST WORTHING 2H 33
West Worthing Station (Rail) 1A 34
West Worthing Tennis & Squash Club
4C 18
Wharf Rd. BN41: Port 4D 26
Wheatfield Way BN2: Brig 5B 14
Wheatlands Cl. BN10: Tel C 2F 39
Wheatsheaf Gdns. BN7: Lew 3G 17
Wheelwright Lodge
BN15: Somp 3A 22
(off West St.)
Whichelo Pl. BN2: Brig 4G 29
Whippingham Rd. BN2: Brig 2G 29
Whippingham St. BN2: Brig 2G 29
Whipping Post La. BN2: Rott 3F 37
Whistler Ct. BN1: Brig 1D 28
Whitebeam Rd. BN13: Durr 5E 19
Whitecross St.
BN1: Brig 2C 44 (4E 29)
WHITEHAWK 4B 30
Whitehawk Cl. BN2: Brig 5A 30
Whitehawk Cres. BN2: Brig 5A 30
Whitehawk Hill Rd. BN2: Brig 5H 29
Whitehawk Rd. BN2: Brig 4A 30
Whitehawk Way BN2: Brig 4B 30
White Hill BN7: Lew 4E 17
White Horse Sq. BN44: Stey 3C 4
White Ho. Pl. BN13: Durr 2G 19
White Lion Ct. *BN43: Shor S 3A 24*
(off Ship St.)
White Lodge BN3: Hove 2A 28
Whitelot Cl. BN42: S'wick 6G 9
Whitelot Way BN42: S'wick 6G 9
Whiterock Pl. BN42: S'wick 3G 25
White St. BN2: Brig 5F 29
White Styles Rd.
BN15: Somp 3H 21
White Styles Ter.
BN15: Somp 3H 21
Whitethorn Dr. BN1: Brig 4H 11
Whiteway Cl. BN25: Sea 1D 42
Whiteway La. BN2: Rott 2G 37
Whittingehame Gdns.
BN1: Brig 5D 12
Whitworth Ho. *BN11: Wor 1B 34*
(off St Botolph's Rd.)
Whylands Av. BN13: Durr 2F 19
Whylands Cl. BN13: Durr 2F 19
Whylands Cres. BN13: Durr 2F 19
Wick Hall BN3: Hove 4B 28
Wickhurst Cl. BN41: Port 6H 9
Wickhurst Ri. BN41: Port 5H 9
Wickhurst Rd. BN41: Port 6H 9
Wicklands Av. BN2: Salt 3A 38
Widdicombe Way BN2: Brig 6A 14
Widewater Cl. BN15: S Lan 5G 23
Widewater Ct. BN43: Shor B 5G 23
Wigmore Cl. BN1: Brig 1F 29
Wigmore Rd. BN14: Broad 4D 20
Wigmore Trad. Est.
BN14: Broad 5F 21
Wilbury Av. BN3: Hove 2H 27
Wilbury Cres. BN3: Hove 3A 28
Wilbury Gdns. BN3: Hove 2A 28
Wilbury Grange BN3: Hove 4A 28
Wilbury Gro. BN3: Hove 4A 28
Wilbury Lodge BN3: Hove 3A 28
Wilbury Mans. *BN3: Hove 2B 28*
(off Wilbury Vs.)
Wilbury Rd. BN3: Hove 4A 28
Wilbury Vs. BN3: Hove 3A 28
Wilby Av. BN42: S'wick 1G 25
Wild Pk. Cl. BN2: Brig 5A 14
Wilfrid Rd. BN3: Hove 2D 26
Wilkinson Cl. BN2: Rott 1F 37
Wilkinson Way BN25: Sea 3D 42
William Morris Ct.
BN14: Broad 6F 21
Williams Rd. BN43: Shor S 2D 24
William St.
BN2: Brig 4D 44 (5E 29)
BN41: Port 3B 26
William Sutton Ho. *BN1: Brig 4C 44*
(off Tichborne St.)
Willingdon Rd. BN2: Brig 1A 30
Willowbrook Pk. BN15: S Lan 5E 23
Willowbrook Rd.
BN14: Broad 6G 21
Willow Cl. BN2: W'dean 2G 31
BN15: S Lan 5G 23
BN44: Stey 2C 4
Willow Ct. BN3: Hove 3B 28
BN11: Wor 1A 34
Willow Cres. BN13: Durr 5E 19
Willow Dr. BN25: Sea 4H 43
Willow Est., The BN9: New 3G 41
Willow Ho. *BN12: Gor S 6C 18*
(off Goring Chase)
Willows, The *BN2: Brig 2F 29*
(off Prince's Cres.)
BN14: Fin 2C 6
BN15: Lan 5C 22
(off Grinstead La.)
BN25: Sea 4D 42
Willow Wlk. BN9: New 3E 41
Wilmington Cl. BN1: Brig 3E 13

A-Z Brighton & Worthing 67

Wilmington Ct.—Zion Gdns.

Wilmington Ct. BN11: Wor 3A 34	Windsor Lodge BN1: Brig 4B 44	Woburn Pl. BN1: Brig 3B 14

WORTHING HOSPITAL 1E 35

Wilmington Ct. BN11: Wor 3A 34
Wilmington Pde. *BN1: Brig* *3D 12*
(off Wilmington Way)
Wilmington Rd. BN9: New 5D 40
BN25: Sea 3C 42
Wilmington Way BN1: Brig 3D 12
Wilmot Ct. *BN43: Shor S* *2E 25*
(off Wilmot Rd.)
Wilmot Rd. BN43: Shor S 2D 24
Wilson Av. BN2: Brig 4B 36
Wiltshire Ho. *BN2: Brig* *5F 29*
(off Lavender St.)
Wimborne Cl. BN11: Wor 2H 33
Winchelsea Cl. BN25: Sea 2G 43
Winchelsea Cl. BN11: Wor 3A 34
Winchelsea Gdns.
BN11: Wor 3H 33
Winchester Ct. BN11: Wor 2B 34
Winchester Ho. *BN12: Gor S* ..*1C 32*
(off Goring St.)
Winchester Rd. BN11: Wor 2B 34
Winchester St. BN1: Brig 2E 29
Wincombe Rd. BN1: Brig 1B 28
Windermere Ct. BN2: Brig 4G 29
BN12: Gor S 2D 32
Windermere Cres.
BN12: Gor S 5F 19
Windlesham Av. BN1: Brig 4C 28
Windlesham Cl. BN41: Port 1A 26
Windlesham Cl. BN1: Brig 1A 44
Windlesham Gdns.
BN1: Brig 1A 44 (4C 28)
BN43: Shor S 2B 24
Windlesham Ho. *BN1: Brig* *4C 28*
(off Windlesham Rd.)
Windlesham Mans.
BN3: Hove *3C 28*
(off Davigdor Rd.)
Windlesham Rd. BN1: Brig 4C 28
Windmill Cl. BN3: Hove 6F 11
BN44: Up B 4G 5
Windmill Dr. BN1: Brig 2A 12
Windmill Pde. BN42: S'wick ...1G 25
Windmill Rd. BN42: S'wick 1G 25
Windmill St. BN2: Brig 4F 29
Windmill Vw. BN1: Brig 2E 13
Windover Cres. BN7: Lew 3C 16
Windrush Cl. BN13: Durr 2E 19
Windsor Bldgs.
BN1: Brig 4B 44 (5D 28)
Windsor Cl. BN3: Hove 5G 11
BN25: Sea 1A 42
Windsor Ct. BN1: Brig 4B 12
(Tongdean La.)
BN1: Brig 4B 44
(Windsor St.)
BN11: Wor 2G 35

Windsor Lodge *BN1: Brig* *4B 44*
(off Windsor St.)
BN2: Brig *5F 29*
(off High St.)
BN3: Hove 4H 27
Windsor Rd. BN11: Wor 1F 35
Windsor St.
BN1: Brig 4B 44 (5D 28)
Windsor Way BN15: S Lan 4F 23
Winfield Av. BN1: Brig 2D 12
Winfield Cl. BN1: Brig 3D 12
BN41: Port 4A 10
Winlesham Rd. BN43: Shor S ..2B 24
Winston Bus. Cen. BN15: Lan ..5A 22
Winston Rd. BN15: Lan 6A 22
Winterbourne Cl. BN7: Lew 5C 16
BN13: Durr 5D 18
Winterbourne Ct. *BN13: Durr* ..*5D 18*
(off Winterbourne Cl.)
Winterbourne Hollow
BN7: Lew 5D 16
Winterbourne La. BN7: Lew 5C 16
(not continuous)
Winterbourne M. BN7: Lew 5D 16
Winterbourne Way
BN13: Durr 5D 18
Winterton Way
BN43: Shor B 4D 24
Winton Av. BN2: Salt 2A 38
Winton Pl. BN11: Wor 1D 34
Wisborough Ct. BN13: W Tar ...4H 19
Wisden Ct. BN14: Fin V 1A 20
Wish Cl. BN3: Hove 2E 27
Wish Rd. BN3: Hove 4E 27
Wiston Av. BN14: Wor 5A 20
Wiston Cl. BN14: Wor 5B 20
Wiston Ct. *BN43: Shor S* *2E 25*
(off Arundel Cl.)
Wiston Rd. BN2: Brig 3B 30
Wiston Way BN2: Brig 3B 30
WITHDEAN 5C 12
Withdean (Park & Ride) 4B 12
Withdean Av. BN1: Brig 6B 12
BN12: Gor S 4D 32
Withdean Cl. BN1: Brig 5C 12
Withdean Cl. BN1: Brig 5B 12
Withdean Cres. BN1: Brig 5C 12
Withdean Hall BN1: Brig 5C 12
Withdean Ri. BN1: Brig 5B 12
Withdean Rd. BN1: Brig 5B 12
Withdean Sports Complex 4B 12
Withdean Stadium 5B 12
Withyham Av. BN2: Salt 3A 38
Withy Patch Caravans
BN15: Lan 2F 23
Wivelsfield Rd. BN2: Salt 1A 38
Woburn Ct. BN11: Wor 2C 34

Woburn Pl. BN1: Brig 3B 14
Wolseley Rd. BN1: Brig 2H 13
BN41: Port 2A 26
Wolsey Pl. BN11: Wor 2A 34
Wolstonbury Rd. BN3: Hove ...3C 28
Wolstonbury Wlk.
BN43: Shor S 1B 24
Wolverstone Dr. BN1: Brig 6G 13
Woodard Rd. BN15: Lan 3D 22
Woodards Vw. BN43: Shor B ...5H 23
Woodbourne Av. BN1: Brig 4D 12
Woodhouse Cl. BN3: Hove 3E 27
Woodhouse Rd. BN3: Hove 3E 27
WOODINGDEAN 2F 31
Woodingdean Bus. Pk.
BN2: W'dean 1F 31
Woodland Av. BN3: Hove 6H 11
BN13: High S 1G 19
Woodland Cl. BN3: Hove 6H 11
Woodland Ct. BN3: Hove 4H 11
Woodland Dr. BN3: Hove 6H 11
Woodland Pde. BN3: Hove 5H 11
Woodlands BN3: Hove 6A 12
Woodlands, The BN1: Brig 3C 12
Woodlands Cl. BN10: Peace ...3F 39
BN13: Clap 1B 18
Woodland Vw. *BN2: Brig* *6C 14*
(off Taunton Rd.)
Woodland Wlk. BN2: O'dean ...6F 31
Woodland Way BN1: Brig 4D 12
Woodlea Rd. BN13: W Tar 6A 20
Woodmancote Rd.
BN14: Wor 6B 20
Woodpecker Way BN13: Durr ...5E 19
Woodruff Av. BN3: Hove 6H 11
Woodsdale Ct. BN14: Broad ...5E 21
Woods Ho. *BN3: Hove* *2G 27*
(off Sackville Rd.)
Woodside Av. BN1: Brig 6B 12
Woodside Lodge BN1: Brig 6B 12
Woodside Rd. BN14: Wor 6B 20
Woods Way BN12: Gor S 1E 33
Woodvale Crematorium
BN2: Brig 2H 29
Woodview BN43: Shor S 1B 24
Woodview Cl. BN1: Brig 2H 13
Woodview Ct. BN43: Shor S ...1C 24
Worcester Ct. *BN1: Brig* *4C 28*
(off Windlesham Rd.)
BN11: Wor *3A 34*
(off Pevensey Gdns.)
Worcester Vs. BN3: Hove 3C 26
Wordsworth Rd. BN11: Wor ...3C 34
Wordsworth St. BN3: Hove 3G 27
WORTHING 2D 34
Worthing Aquarena 2F 35
Worthing Crematorium
BN14: Fin 1A 6

WORTHING HOSPITAL 1E 35
Worthing Leisure Cen. 1G 33
Worthing Mus. & Art Gallery ..2D 34
Worthing Pier 3E 35
Worthing Station (Rail) 1D 34
Wraysbury Gdns. BN15: Lan ...3C 22
Wychwood Gdns.
BN11: Wor 1H 35
Wyck Ct. *BN41: Port* *3A 26*
(off St Aubyn's Rd.)
Wyckham La. BN44: Stey 1D 4
Wye Ho. BN11: Wor 2B 34
Wyke Av. BN11: Wor 2E 35
Wykeham Cl. BN44: Stey 3C 4
Wykeham Rd. BN11: Wor 2C 34
Wykeham Ter.
BN1: Brig 4B 44 (5D 28)
Wyndham St. BN2: Brig 6F 29
Wynnes M. BN3: Hove 3G 27
Wyvern Ct. *BN11: Wor* *3C 34*
(off West St.)

Yardley St. BN1: Brig 2E 29
Yarrow Rd. BN7: Lew 3D 16
Yeoman Rd. BN13: Durr 5D 18
Yeomans Ga. BN12: Gor S 6D 18
Yeomans Way BN13: Durr 6D 18
Yew Tree Cl. BN15: Lan 5C 22
York Av. BN3: Hove 4C 28
York Ct. *BN3: Hove* *3C 28*
(off Nizells Av.)
York Gro. BN1: Brig 1A 44 (3D 28)
York Hill BN1: Brig 1C 44 (3E 29)
York Ho. *BN41: Port* *2A 26*
(off Crown Rd.)
Yorklands BN3: Hove 4H 11
York Mans. *BN3: Hove* *4C 28*
(off York Av.)
York Pl. BN1: Brig 2D 44 (4E 29)
BN3: Hove *4C 28*
(off York Av.)
York Rd. BN3: Hove 4C 28
BN10: Peace 5A 40
BN11: Wor 2E 35
York Vs. BN1: Brig 1A 44 (3D 28)
Youngsmere Cl. BN1: Brig 2F 13

Zion Gdns. BN1: Brig ...4B 44 (5D 28)

The representation on the maps of a road, track or footpath is no evidence of the existence of a right of way.

The Grid on this map is the National Grid taken from Ordnance Survey® mapping with the permission of the Controller of Her Majesty's Stationery Office.

Copyright of Geographers' A-Z Map Company Ltd.

No reproduction by any method whatsoever of any part of this publication is permitted without the prior consent of the copyright owners.

SAFETY CAMERA INFORMATION

Safety camera locations are publicised by the Safer Roads Partnership who operate them in order to encourage drivers to comply with speed limits at these sites. It is the driver's absolute responsibility to be aware of and to adhere to speed limits at all times.

By showing this safety camera information it is the intention of Geographers' A-Z Map Company Ltd., to encourage safe driving and greater awareness of speed limits and vehicle speed. Data accurate at time of printing.